CAD/CAM IN CLOTHING AND TEXTILES

❖

CAD/CAM IN CLOTHING AND TEXTILES

❖

Stephen Gray

Gower

Published by
Gower Publishing Limited
Gower House
Croft Road
Aldershot
Hampshire GU11 3HR
England

Gower
Old Post Road
Brookfield
Vermont 05036
USA

British Library Cataloguing in Publication Data
Gray, Stephen
 CAD/CAM in clothing and textiles
 1. CAD/CAM systems 2. Textile industry – Data processing
 3. Clothing trade – Data processing
 I. Title II. Design Council
 677'.00285

ISBN 0 566 07673 X

Library of Congress Cataloging-in-Publication Data
Gray, Stephen (Stephen Nicholas), 1954–
    CAD/CAM in clothing and textiles/Stephen Gray.
    p.cm.
    Includes index.
    ISBN 0-566-07673-X
    1. Clothing trade – Data processing. 2. Textile industry – Data processing. 3. Computer-aided design. I. Title.
    TT497.G75 1998
    687'.0285–dc21   97–45182 CIP

Typeset in Derby by Saxon Graphics Ltd and printed in Great Britain by Biddles Ltd, Guildford.

To my grandfather, Stuart Hill, who died during the writing of this book: thank you for being so special.

CONTENTS

❖

FIGURES

❖

TABLES

❖

ACKNOWLEDGEMENTS

❖

Two people deserve special mention and have my gratitude and love: Susie for her continual support and understanding and my mother for her ceaseless care and meticulous proofreading.

My editor, Suzie Duke, must also be thanked: she has provided great encouragement and support and has tempered this with great patience at every missed deadline!

1

A BACKGROUND TO CAD/CAM

❖

INTRODUCTION

Computer-aided design (CAD) and computer-aided manufacture (CAM) are terms that have become synonymous with a change in working practice in many companies in the clothing and textiles industry. This book aims to explain some of the features and benefits of CAD/CAM systems and to assist clothing and textiles companies (manufacturers, suppliers and retailers) in the task of integrating CAD/CAM with other computer technologies.

The clothing and textiles industry is always looking for new ideas for promotion and presentation. It is continually striving for quicker response in a market that is demanding better choice, higher quality and greater style. Computers (in the form of CAD/CAM systems) have been making a significant contribution to the production flow through manufacturing companies since the early 1970s.

The relationship between the designers, manufacturers and retailers is complex but is based on a common interest in the production of commercially viable designs. It is difficult to think of another industry where there is such a clear link between the supplier of raw materials and the buyer of the finished goods, and CAD/CAM systems are now used throughout the supply chain.

Yarns and fibres are used to produce fabrics which in turn are made into garments. CAD systems can simulate both the colour and structure of yarns to create realistic fabric images. Samples can be created on screen without the need to manufacture products. The design of each fabric incorporates the properties of the fibres and the design of each garment requires an understanding of the fabrics used in its creation. Clothing designs can be created from scanned images of real materials or from electronic versions

1

imported from other CAD systems. In addition to the essential artistic design skills there is a lot of science involved in the creation of successful clothes: CAD can assist in the creation of pattern shapes and the development of new sizes. New fibres give new design possibilities – just think of the effect that Lycra® has made on the fashion market and consider the use that is being made of microfibres: in the more sophisticated systems allowances for different material properties can be incorporated into designs creating a more realistic 'look and feel'.

The immediate benefits that CAD/CAM systems offer are a reduction in lead times, a lowering of direct costs and improved communications with customers and suppliers. Many people think that CAD/CAM is appropriate only to larger businesses and penetration of systems into smaller companies in the industry is still minimal (for example a 1995 report showed that less than 10 per cent of companies in Nottinghamshire had invested in the technology). However, the general reduction in the price of computers coupled with the availability of effective, inexpensive software has made systems much more attractive to smaller companies and the biggest growth in the use of CAD/CAM is likely to come from this sector.

CAD/CAM systems allow users to offer a more flexible and responsive service to customers and can therefore contribute to developing businesses. Smaller companies often survive on their versatility and the increasing pressure from the retail market for a quick response business partnership with its suppliers means that computer systems are needed by all levels of the industry.

DEFINITION OF TERMS

CAD/CAM is the abbreviated form of two concepts, computer-aided design and computer-aided manufacture, which are simply what they say – computer *aids* for the designer and manufacturer. The two terms are often used interchangeably or together but there is an important division: CAD is generally used to support the creative processes in the design studio and CAM is used in the manufacturing process to control machinery or systems (such as grading, lay planning or pattern cutting). The first two letters of each acronym must not be ignored: the technology is used to assist in design and manufacturing processes – it is not a replacement for people, nor does it perform work automatically and it is most certainly not a way of solving existing management, organizational or quality problems.

Computer-aided design means different things to different people: a fashion designer would use a CAD system in the manipulation of pattern shapes, a knitwear designer would expect to create stitch structures and a textile designer would use CAD to create multiple colourways of a design. All three could use CAD in the creation of fashion illustrations.

The definition of computer-aided manufacture is straightforward: computer systems can be used to control all sorts of different machinery and processes. Automatic cloth cutters, knitting machines and electronic looms may all be regarded as CAM systems. Each requires a computer to control the moving parts and to pass the instructions from the user to the machinery.

To use the term properly a CAD/CAM system is one where information can be input and manipulated at the design stage and then output to a manufacturing process without the need for information to be produced in paper, cardboard or any other non-electronic form as a means of linking the two together.

CAD is not just for the design room: using it throughout a company can pay dividends in productivity and communication. Similarly, CAM is not just for production: systems have an influence on the entire company from the receipt of raw materials to the dispatch of finished goods. It is only within the contextual view of the whole business that CAD/CAM requirements can sensibly be assessed. This implies the need for significant management understanding and involvement in the introduction of the technology to enable potential users to produce an accurate brief covering their real needs for streamlining their business.

WHAT CAD/CAM CAN OFFER

The three main features of any CAD/CAM system are flexibility, productivity and storage capacity. Flexibility is an increasingly important requirement for a company to survive in the competitive market of the late twentieth century and therefore any tools that help businesses to offer their customers a versatile device are essential. CAD/CAM systems allow designs to be adapted and changed throughout the design and production process. Often systems are so versatile that they increase pressure on managers to improve the supply chain within an organization, ensuring that materials are available on the factory floor for immediate assembly and dispatch. They are capable of providing significantly more output in any unit of time than is possible by purely manual methods and therefore are a positive aid to productivity. Since electronic data can be stored on devices like magnetic disks, tapes or CDs they require minimal storage space, offering great advantages over traditional media which are frequently kept in paper or cardboard form.

The very nature of CAD/CAM systems offers inherent flexibility. Styles can be recalled from libraries, manipulated, graded according to a variety of size charts and then laid out in a cutting plan in a matter of minutes. New fabrics can be designed: woven and knitted structures can be shown on a computer screen hours before samples can be produced on looms or knitting machines. Packaging can be customized by changing labels, typefaces, colours and logos ready for approval within a couple of hours.

Since changes can be made on screen in just seconds CAD systems allow users to save significant time on labour intensive tasks like producing multiple colourways of a fabric design or working out the seam allowances for pleated skirts. Output is frequently made to a colour printer or a pen plotter but there is an increasing move towards paperless communications where data is transferred in electronic form – for example to a laser engraver, electronic knitting machine or automatic fabric cutter. Using computer systems to measure efficiency of cutting patterns (the marker making process) allows managers to determine economically viable levels of cloth wastage thereby providing a control on direct material costs. Throughout the design and manufacturing process 'snapshots' of the current state of any product can be made by interrogating the computer systems. A more accurate overview of the development path can be obtained and therefore requests from customers and demands on suppliers can be expressed more clearly and with greater understanding.

A host of other benefits also exist. It is generally much easier to set and maintain consistent standards at all stages in the design and production process using CAD/CAM systems. These standards in turn lead to improved quality of product and the processes used in its creation, providing the basis for corporate accreditation under standards like ISO 9000. Often designers using CAD have more time to research their ideas since the labour intensive activities are no longer occupying their time. A general increase in research time leads both to better product and to increased market awareness, providing further opportunities for new product development. Sometimes the technology itself provides benefits as it can be used to present ideas in new ways (for example the use of a multimedia slide show employing music, special effects and a commentary to replace a series of montages pasted on to Styrofoam). Clever companies are starting to exploit the technology to heighten their market profile and create an image of a high-tech organization well-versed in computer understanding. Many use telephone links to transfer data in electronic form between sites, thereby avoiding any mistakes in transcription and ensuring timely availability of information in the appropriate location. There is, however, an increasing need to reduce further the response time from concept to sale and the interconnection of the three main parties in a collaborative telecommunications environment heralds a new age in competitiveness, quality and personalization of clothing.

A BRIEF HISTORY OF CAD/CAM SYSTEMS

Unlike many other industries the world of clothing and textiles has been slow to capitalize on new technology, especially in the design room. There are many reasons for this, not least of which is the criticism that the medium is sterile and lacks the tactile appeal of traditional methods. On the other hand the benefits that can be derived from computers are increasingly leading companies to use the technology as a means of survival. Increased use is helping to drive developments in software and hardware, and newer tools have significant creative capabilities in addition to providing the well-documented labour saving processes.

The use of CAD/CAM systems in clothing began only in the early 1970s: the first applications were used to design 'lay plans' – templates showing how pattern pieces will be cut out of cloth, minimizing the amount of waste material that inevitably occurs. This application grew as direct links were made from the lay planning computer terminals to automatic cutting machines. Two companies – Gerber from the USA and Lectra from France – pioneered these first lay planning systems. Inevitably (because they were designed before the days of the PC) they were based on monolithic computer technology and were large and expensive. Since the clothing industry was at that time geared to large production runs (remember when Marks and Spencer had the same goods in its shops all winter?) many companies could justify the cost of lay planning systems on the basis of reduced fabric costs and the ability to repeat and modify existing cutting plans (or 'markers').

As the use of computer systems increased a second range of functions was added to the basic lay planning capability – the making of all the different sizes of a garment, a process known as 'grading'. The justification for adding this process was time saving – grading a seven-piece ladies blouse across six sizes (8, 10, 12, 14, 16 and 18) can take up to 12 hours by hand and about 2 hours by computer. Over a 15-year period (until the debut of the IBM personal computer) the number of grading and lay planning systems in the UK grew to a user base of about 200. The companies that installed this technology were almost exclusively the larger manufacturers.

Systems for the control of knitting and weaving machinery were developed and these too were installed in the larger companies. The majority were created by the machinery manufacturers and the software they offered mixed the practical elements of machine control and the aesthetic representation of design. They were generally complex to use and were frequently operated by competent technicians who interpreted designers' ideas. Justification for their use centred on the simplicity of transfer of design into fabric combined with the ability to make changes throughout the design process. This operating method is still commonplace but there is now a trend towards 'designer technicians': people who understand both technology and aesthetics.

Designers in the clothing and textiles industry were slow to appreciate the power and sophistication of computer graphics systems. The first commercial applications in fashion began in the late 1980s with the use of the CDI system by Courtaulds and by Coats Viyella. This is somewhat surprising as computer-aided manufacturing systems had been widely used since the early 1970s but it is indicative of the division between design and production in so many companies. The CDI system cost over £100 000 and included options for pseudo-3D design and for textile design (knit and weave). It was specifically geared to the clothing market and had many of the features required by this industry and not by others. Its primary use was in scanning information (existing artwork, photographs or textiles) and modifying images to create new versions. The system was rarely used for original design creation and many considered the functions it offered both inflexible and cumbersome.

More recently there have been a number of software packages aimed at the graphic design market. Many of these appeal to the clothing and textiles designer too. Generically the functions within a computer 'paintbox' mimic those in the real world but they also include many features that can be achieved only with electronic technology. The use of computer paintbox systems for original design work is still in its infancy – many textile designers find it difficult to believe that an image need not exist in 'original' form on existing media before it can be entered into a computer system. However, a number of enterprising designers are starting to exploit their understanding of the technology combined with their own artistic talents to create completely computer-based designs.

Due to the relatively low cost of PCs, the number of businesses that can afford CAD/CAM has expanded and its use can be seen in all sizes of company from the one-person design studio to the multi-site corporation. In recent years the traditional functions of machinery control, marker making and grading have all been rewritten to function on smaller computers and novel design functions for patterns and textiles have been added. The use of personal computer technology has meant that other functions like the creation of documentation, labels and packaging can all be performed on a single terminal, often by a single user.

As the influence of the PC and the Apple Mac grew in the late 1980s the suppliers of the large systems noticed a trend towards the use of small systems for original design work. A wealth of software aimed primarily at graphic design appeared and captivated those designers who could see its application in the fashion market. Competition from this mass market caused the clothing and textiles system suppliers to re-evaluate their products and markets and most now offer systems for design as well as production, sometimes fully integrated and sometimes as separate, but compatible, units.

Since the late 1980s rapid progress has been made by users and many businesses now rely heavily on computer-aided design tools. CAD/CAM suppliers have responded to the enthusiasm generated in the market and have been steadily refining their products bringing out more and more functions designed specifically for the fashion market.

DRIVING FORCES BEHIND CAD/CAM SYSTEMS

Demographic trends form an important part of any company's thinking and as the population gets older and larger there are increasing pressures on designers to adapt their ideas for different sectors of the market. This adaptation process is often easily performed on CAD/CAM systems without the need to go back to the drawing board. Competition, especially from low labour cost countries, is an ever-present threat and many businesses are responding by increasing the design content of their products, using quality and responsiveness as additional tools in the fight for market share. Computer technology can assist greatly in their work. Some of the now inherent versatility in companies was created during the economic recession of the late 1980s and early 1990s. The recession had a dramatic impact on many companies and those unable to change their ways of working, their products or their quality and delivery were forced out of business. Many of the survivors attribute some of their success to sensible use of CAD/CAM systems as a positive aid to design, planning and production.

The nature of the clothing retail market has changed dramatically over the last 20 years – no longer do shops maintain a standard range of goods for an entire season. Instead they keep as small a stock as possible and rely on the flexibility of the manufacturers and designers to produce goods in a timely and efficient manner. The customer is also demanding a greater variety of improved quality goods representing better 'value for money'. Market forces are therefore driving the industry to manufacture efficiently, quickly and with more flexibility. This in turn reflects the need for good design and quick response throughout the supply chain.

There is quite a difference between the markets for mainstream clothing and high fashion. CAD/CAM has been used only by the former industry (which makes large quantities of each product) and is unlikely to be needed or even wanted by the high fashion industry (making very small quantities of exclusive items) except possibly for novelty value. The majority of the 9000 UK companies are producing for the mainstream clothing, furnishing and interiors market. Their output is driven by the retail sector and everyone measures success in 'best sellers'. This is not by any means the only judgement criterion but is undoubtedly an essential indicator: quality, price, aesthetic quality, handle and so forth are all elements that contribute to the success of a garment. One thing is certain: a bad design will not sell!

SEASONAL WORK

Every country in the world has a clothing industry. It is not uncommon for goods to be designed in one country, manufactured in a second and sold in a third. The industry is often regarded as a low-technology sector yet it produces millions of goods at highly competitive prices for a volatile market. It is a massive user of information, much of it in picture form. The driving force is the seasonal nature of the business with the main changes in climate (spring/summer and autumn/winter) demanding completely new ranges of garments in the stores.

The clothing and textiles industry designs for at least two (and often four or more) seasons each year, requiring studios to produce increasing numbers of new ideas for products that will be in the shops for only a short period. Retailers demand good designs enhanced by quality, originality and flexibility, and this puts pressure on the designers to produce better ideas, greater variety and improved styling. A trend towards higher design content can be seen throughout Europe in small volumes of well-designed, high quality products. This is especially true in highly fashion conscious countries like Italy and France. In the UK the 'designer' industry increased by 60 per cent between 1991 and 1994 with much of the frivolity of 'fashion' garments replaced by well-designed collections tempered with sound business practice.

Retailers have to guess what the market will buy, have to assess trends for colours and styles and have to communicate these ideas to their suppliers. In turn suppliers have to design within these limitations, have to source fabrics, trimmings and accessories and have to be able to manufacture quickly and to a high standard. The fabric producers have similar problems: they have to use all their experience and knowledge to mix traditional techniques and materials with new ideas and yarns to manufacture cloth with aesthetic appeal and practical application.

Customers are influenced by the media: TV, magazines, films and the press. Trends in the economy, events in politics, the weather and issues about the environment all affect the consumer and all have to be considered by the designer. The clothing market needs to react quickly to all these influences and retailers do not want to be left with large quantities of unwanted garments in their stores. The timing of an introduction of new goods is also critical – in a seasonal industry such as clothing everyone is aware of the important times and dates of shows, seasons and sales.

QUICK RESPONSE

Retail pressures in the British clothing and textiles industry are driving designers and manufacturers down a 'quick response' path. This pressure has been a significant influence in the decision to use computer systems to streamline production and to enhance presentation and design. The scope of computer technology spreads much further than design and production: with modern communications technology systems can be linked together to provide a wealth of data to a variety of users, each with differing needs and expectations.

The demands of the clothing industry for CAD/CAM systems have been growing for some time as a reaction to the increasing need for quick response at all stages in the design, manufacturing and retail process. Retailers are directly responsible for demanding quick response from their manufacturers. To minimize their stock and to react quickly to market trends they require their suppliers to produce goods very quickly and to high quality standards. Market forces are the reasons for the change in retailers' practices. Customers are demanding better quality (in fabrics, manufacturing standards and fit), more variety and improved value for money. This is true across the entire age spectrum from childhood to old-age and the retailers are forever catering to client needs.

The growing trend in manufacturing industry towards low volumes, greater variety and a quicker response is forcing companies to rethink their work patterns to keep up with stiff competition, especially from abroad.

The clothing and textiles industry is undoubtedly market-led. This means that changes in styles, sizes, fabrics and packaging are commonplace and a manufacturer unable to supply goods in this quick response manner is unable to compete effectively. Large and small companies need to understand information technology to compete seriously in the international arena. A primary reason why the UK clothing and textile industry is (portrayed as being) in constant decline is due to businesses ignoring new technology or failing to exploit its full potential.

CAD/CAM is one way in which a quicker response to market demands can be achieved whilst maintaining high quality. To ensure the maximum benefits from the technology, essential steps need to be taken to install the right system at the right price for the right reasons. CAD/CAM will benefit businesses that allow themselves to be educated in the technology.

Suppliers know that it is impossible to manufacture quickly without sources of materials (fabrics, trims and accessories) also available on a quick response basis. The demands of the customers are placing strict disciplines on all elements of the manufacturing supply chain: quick response is essential at all points in the design/manufacture/retail structure. Fabrics need to be produced in smaller batch sizes but in increasing varieties of colours and weights. These need to be co-ordinated with garment designs, accessories and trims. The use of information technology is the only means by which true quick response can be achieved, passing information between systems and processes both inter and intra company.

The ways of the market are led by the retailers – many will set themes at the beginning of a season's design work (remembering that they work about one year in advance of the goods being available in the market). Designers further back in the supply chain need to react to these requirements, producing garments and textiles sympathetic to the retailers' needs. The use of CAD/CAM is increasing fast and its acceptance amongst the design community is being driven by the availability of many exciting new software facilities and rapid improvements in screen and printer quality.

Designers can use CAD to produce multiple colourways, pattern repeats and colour separations, which are commonly regarded as time-consuming tasks using conventional media. The CAD tool can ease the workload without replacing the design talents. Clothing and textile designers are starting to use CAD systems as another set of tools alongside paints, inks and crayons. Initially many designers saw computers as a threat – replacing creativity by mechanization – but experience has shown that they can enhance creativity by removing many of the tedious tasks from a designer's load, affording more time to experiment with new ideas. CAD is being used as one way in which modification time can be reduced. It also encourages designers to experiment and enables them to produce 'mock-up' photographic pictures showing garments that have never been made. It can even be used to produce sample packaging and display material.

Many of the larger retailers (Marks and Spencer, Next, Debenhams, etc.) require vast numbers of designs, samples and costings before a buying decision is made. There is frequent need for a number of iterations around the design/presentation/costing loop, each costing time and money. CAD has an increasing role as a presentation tool in its own right. A few designers are even working with the buyers on the CAD screen to explore options before hard copy prints are made, thereby reducing the number of changes required to a minimal level. This practice, which appeals to the whole psychology of buying and selling, can only improve communications and therefore is set to grow.

GLOBAL MARKETS

Textile designers need to work closely with the consumers of their product and there is great opportunity for CAD to be used as the means of communication between them and the designers of clothing, furniture and home interiors. Clothing designers can use CAD systems to record and recall libraries of patterns and sizes so that garments can be altered in line with retailers' needs with minimal effort.

Good design is independent of origin, and the efficiency of transferring information from design room to factory is critical to business success. Today's technology can send information on colour, style and size via a telephone line anywhere in the world in a matter of minutes to be used as the basis for manufacturing in the global market. This information is precise, controlled and guarantees that recipients are able to interpret it within their own environment, rather than having to rely on poor drawings. The use of the technology as a means of communication helps companies to avoid mistakes, removes the need for duplication of tasks and assists in the reduction of costs and development timescales.

THE COST OF CAD/CAM

It is a simple fact that clothing items are of generally low value and are relatively cheap to produce. As such the amount costed for design into each sale is minimal and the industry has generally functioned on large volumes of goods to cover design costs. As production runs become increasingly small in volume and ever more varied there is a need to charge a higher per-item figure for design. Used sensibly, CAD/CAM will reduce the amount of labour involved in each design and it can therefore contribute to cost savings and justify its purchase.

Many businesses are still put off by the perceived high cost of computer technology but CAD is now priced at a level that even freelance designers can afford. CAD/CAM has many benefits but the financial value of installing it is difficult to quantify and requires a full assessment of all costs. Some of the cost savings achievable through CAD/CAM include a reduction in media and photocopying, an improvement in colour consistency and ability to meet deadlines. The use of CAD saves time and this can be used productively by designers for greater experimentation, sometimes producing ideas for new markets. The use of high quality presentation material helps to communicate these ideas to potential clients. In Chapter 5 the true costs of CAD/CAM are discussed together with an indication of the opportunities that may be lost by not investing.

Computers are not able to offer solutions to problems of poor management, badly structured companies or low quality standards. In the past some businesses invested in CAD/CAM systems in the hope that they would provide answers to endemic problems. Others bought computers for tasks such as stock control, invoicing or production control. In most of these cases the payback is questionable. A 1994 survey by management consultants Touche Ross revealed that, *with the exception of CAD*, few enterprises believed that computer systems were having a significant impact on business performance. The study investigated the use of IT systems in 320 of the larger companies; of these 44 per cent used CAD and nearly all planned to extend its use. It is seen as a substantial contributor to competitiveness with improved quality, better presentations and reduced lead time to manufacture being cited as positive elements.

In the following chapters the application of CAD and CAM to different parts of the clothing and textiles industry is discussed and examples that demonstrate payback and novel approaches to the technology are included. The ways in which commercial opportunities can be created by users of the technology are outlined and it is hoped that readers will be able to use the material to inform their own planning process. Investment in CAD/CAM should be viewed as significantly more than an insurance policy for survival: used well it will become an essential ingredient for success and expansion.

Computer hardware and software is evolving fast and telecommunications providers are offering ever more capability to link suppliers and customers electronically, so the book ends with a glimpse into the future.

The book takes the reader through the diverse ways in which CAD/CAM systems are used for both design origination and production. It then outlines the justification that companies should adopt before investing in hardware and software and identifies suppliers and systems. An indication of the true cost of systems follows the selection process as an aid to the investment decision process.

People are not left out of the consideration and Chapter 6 concentrates on human issues associated with the use of information technology. Recognizing that CAD/CAM installations are not the only computer systems in companies, the next chapter covers the ways in which they can be integrated with other products and services. The rate of change of technology continues apace and CAD/CAM systems will always perform best on the latest hardware; Chapter 8 examines the current state of the art in software and telecommunications to show how new functionality can be added to configurations in any organization.

As the clothing and textiles industry adopts the technology its impact will have an increasingly beneficial effect on cost, quality and variety. The final chapter of the book considers how future developments are likely to occur and how they will affect different types of CAD/CAM user.

2

HOW CAD/CAM
SYSTEMS ARE USED

❖

All the big names in the clothing market use CAD/CAM systems – SR Gent, Coats Viyella, Courtaulds, Desmonds, Dewhirsts and so on are users and enthusiastic supporters of the technology. All the main suppliers to Marks and Spencer (together with a host of smaller ones) use CAD. M&S itself uses CAD to select colour palettes, to prepare presentation and packaging material and to design pattern blocks. Other big retailers use the technology in their own design studios and there is a strong drive towards the use of CAD as the means of communication with their suppliers. Small companies, too, are starting to use the technology as an integral part of their business.

Used properly CAD/CAM systems offer distinct commercial advantages to all companies in the clothing and textiles supply chain. Large and small businesses will be left behind if they do not embrace the capabilities that computer technology in general and CAD/CAM in particular can offer.

THE SUPPLY CHAIN

Because CAD/CAM can assist in the streamlining of the link between design and production it can make a significant contribution to the quick response demands of the retailers and, linked to flexible manufacturing techniques, it can improve the efficiency, responsiveness and market position of the user company. Those companies with comprehensive database facilities are even able to link designers to information on costing, allowing them to adjust their ideas to fit price guidelines without the need to finish their work before costing can begin.

All retailers need to minimize their investment in stock and they now have a philosophy that demands a highly interactive relationship with their manufacturers. Orders are much smaller, have more variations and have to be delivered fast. A 'quick response' retail market, reflecting directly the buying patterns of you and me, the customers, demands quick response manufacture and this in turn relies on quick response design and quick response supply.

CAD systems allow users to make changes quickly – new versions of designs can be produced in minutes. Those companies using the technology find that they can meet the time requirements of the retailers in the design studio and some have used the technology to integrate the manufacturing and design processes using electronic links to transfer information in an efficient, reliable and accurate manner. The clothing and textiles industry well understands the intimate links that exist between the producers of yarns and the manufacturers of fabrics, the designers of garments and the suppliers of materials, the retailers and their manufacturers. In all of these establishments there is a potential user of CAD/CAM and in many there is a real need for other types of information technology.

CAD is often used as the basis for interaction between individuals involved in the supply chain: manufacturers produce garment ideas, packaging and merchandising suggestions directly out of CAD packages and fabric manufacturers can produce computer simulations of their products to enable customers to make buying decisions before samples have been produced. Some retailers even design shop floor layouts on CAD systems. Indeed, as the use of CAD becomes increasingly standard practice there is an opportunity for ideas to be delivered in electronic form (down a telephone line, via a floppy disk or on CD-ROM) as the primary means of transport, saving waste and offering instant results. This will help to reduce the amount of time spent producing unnecessary samples and will minimize the amount of time taken from concept to finished goods.

CAD systems themselves are often used in isolation and they come in many different configurations, each geared to a specific niche in the market. To explore these ideas it is easiest to start with an indication of the ways in which systems are used in different parts of the supply chain.

DESIGN

Textile designers of all kinds use CAD: its influence spreads from raw material production to retail outlet. It has a wide range of applications from the representation of colour combinations to original design and illustration. Some designers use it as a substitute for repetitive tasks, others as a creative medium in its own right. The extensive functions allow it to create images from the abstract to the photographic, and graphical effects can be used in an imaginative manner to heighten their use as a means of communication. Its practical use also covers the creation of supporting items like merchandising and display material, swing tickets and packaging.

Clothing designers use CAD systems to perform the time-consuming functions of block modification, employing the wide range of geometric functions to slice, pleat, move darts, lengthen or shorten, add or remove pleats and tucks and so on. All of these tasks can be performed with or without seam allowance and many systems allow users to measure joins to indicate whether or not the results will sew together correctly. Output to pen plotters is generally used to create paper templates which are used as the guide to cutting, first in one-off quantities for sample making and then in multiples for production, when a marker will be created according to the ratios required by the customer. In addition to these design functions CAD is used to grade patterns according to a variety of methods, each of which is linked (usually via a grade rule library) to a size chart. These functions are performed in a fraction of the time taken by manual methods and are frequently used as the link between design and production.

MANUFACTURE

CAM is used extensively in the control of fabric production machinery (be it for knitted, woven or printed textiles) as well as for the cutting process in garment manufacture. In many companies CAM systems are used independently of any CAD facility, their justification being made on efficiency, accuracy and cost.

CAM systems are usually operated by specially trained staff, many of whom require significant technical knowledge as well as a good understanding of the product and its component parts. In knitting, for example, technicians require a comprehensive knowledge of stitch structure, yarn tension and needle operation. Weaving machine operators need to understand yarn properties and fabric structure, and garment cutters must appreciate fabric grain and pattern assembly.

For many companies the cost of a CAD/CAM system is determined by the machinery being used for output: a fabric cutter will be more than 70 per cent of the overall price of any system and similar figures are true for knitting machines and looms. In the production environment CAD/CAM systems are used as an integral part of the manufacturing process; machinery has to earn its keep and they are expected to be productive throughout the working day.

TEXTILE DESIGN

Much of the use of CAD grew from the idea that new textiles could be created by scanning existing designs and making modifications. Most of the first systems were used in this manner, some of them to great effect. Problems about colour matching and colour reduction (scanned images always contain too many colours) have been appreciated and worked around. Another approach grew from the idea that it is possible to use the computer as a creative tool in its own right, the starting point for a design being a blank screen. An increasing number of textile designers appreciate the power of CAD when used for original design, especially as it can be used to develop ideas quickly and without risk – at any stage a design can be stored so that multiple derivations can be made from the same base idea.

Textile designers use CAD/CAM systems for three main areas of their work:

O   Design
O   Presentation
O   Production

Within each of these areas every designer will have his or her own speciality and no two users of a system will operate it in identical ways. There are different systems for each of the three main sectors of the market and each has unique features.

KNITTING

Knitting systems allow users to divide illustrations into grids that indicate each stitch and then to specify the structure of the resulting pattern, mixing the combination of coloured yarns and different stitch formations. Some give a realistic visualization of the finished effect on screen, allowing designers to make changes before samples are produced. All have the ability to produce output on tape, disk or by direct connection to knitting machinery so the production of the design is very quick. Designs can then be passed on to production in ready-to-use form.

CAD systems are used for two main purposes: one is to define on a grid format the layout of yarns and stitch formations that will be used to create a final item. In this form CAD is the primary means by which a design is turned into a manufacturable fabric. The other purpose is to produce realistic images that represent the finished product.

Output from systems takes two forms: predominantly systems are used to produce instructions for knitting machinery on floppy disk, magnetic tape or even by direct electronic link. The alternate form of output is via a colour printer on to paper for recording a design or even demonstrating how a garment will look in its made-up form using the basic simulation functions of the computer system.

WEAVING

As with knitting systems woven textile producers can take illustrations and can manipulate colours to represent different threads and structures.

Different effects can be created for the different woven structures (Jacquard, Dobby, etc.) and systems offer users the ability to specify the density of the cloth (in picks and ends) and to allocate colours to each thread. Special effects like brushing the fabric are easily achieved and therefore designers can produce the look of any idea with minimal cost and time. The primary design feature of a CAD system used for weaving is the means by which fabrics can be simulated on screen so that design decisions can be made without the need for sampling. Since sampling is such an expensive process the benefits of CAD are immediately realized, even if they save only the initial samples, users still demanding 'real' textiles to assess quality and handle properties. Good ideas can then be produced on disk, in PROM (Programmable Read Only Memory) or computer chip, on magnetic tape or via direct electronic connection to a suitable loom for weaving into the required fabric. Even the older types of loom can have microchip controllers fitted to control the lifting of the threads during the production process.

PRINT

Printed textile designers have a wealth of systems available to them. Tools for the creation and manipulation of ideas are powerful and effective. Montages can be built and different layers moved and combined to experiment with different effects. Final results can be divided into the appropriate layers for printing (if the traditional mask process is adopted) or can be divided into blocks for four-colour printing. Total control over an image is possible and, unlike manual methods, ideas can be developed in a multiplicity of ways without destroying the original artwork. This tends to make designers less precious with their good ideas and often releases more creative energy because designers are less worried about the time it would take to re-create an original piece.

Generally users of textile design systems start with work created on paper or other medium. Most companies making printed textiles use scanners to capture this data in digital form. They then use CAD systems to manipulate the image, changing colours, adding, deleting, moving or copying elements and putting the overall design into a suitable pattern repeat. A few designers use the medium as a creative tool in its own right, creating images using the digitizing pen and tablet. Others use the scanner's surface as the base for collages, creating images from a variety of objects and using the scanner's operation as another medium. Software packages now have a wide range of effects such as chalk, water-colour and oil which enable different results to be created with the same input devices. Of course, the great advantage is that a user can 'undo' any element so that mistakes or unwanted effects can instantly be corrected. Other systems use digital cameras as a means of data capture – the big advantage of these systems is their ability to represent different lighting conditions.

The same methods are used by designers of woven or knitted textiles, though they often have to be significantly more disciplined than those who create printed fabric as they can use only a limited number of colours. Over and above the basic design functions the more sophisticated knit and weave systems offer simulation possibilities so that users can see the effect of structure and stitch formation on screen, prior to sampling. This is a very powerful facility and often designs can be sold from computer-generated images.

Some CAD systems allow users to create pseudo-3D effects by providing tools to distort two-dimensional fabrics and overlay them on photographic images so that shadows remain. The net result (sometimes called 'two and a half dimensions') gives the impression of photographed clothes in a variety of fabrics. The procedure involves a user tracing the outline of the garment on top of the photograph and then using the computer tools to distort the fabric to fit each panel. Although this takes some time it has the great advantage of being a one-off task and when complete any 2D fabric can be superimposed on the image.

Output from print systems generally tends to be in hard copy form on paper or even directly on to fabric. There is, however, an increasing trend to use the computer as the transfer medium and many laser engraving systems can now accept direct input from floppy disks or CDs. It is obvious that one of the main benefits of the technology is its ability to let users experiment with colour combinations and fabric structures without the need to use production machinery to create samples that will simply be rejected. CAD/CAM systems can, of course, only create images of fabrics – seen through the computer screen or on paper they lack the tactile qualities of real samples – and therefore do not eliminate the need for actual materials; they simply minimize the number that are produced.

For these reasons and others there has been an increasing use of CAD/CAM systems to simulate fabrics and nowadays the quality of prints emerging is so high that they are convincing representations even close-up. All they lack is tactile quality. Some users are so capable that they introduce small imperfections into their designs, reflecting the characteristics of flexibility in the fabrics that they will eventually produce. Hard copy (printed) output is still needed, largely by the buyer, and therefore accurate colour matching is critical.

COLOUR AND PRINTING

The process of transferring designs on to paper involves a colour matching process whereby users indicate the cross-reference between a colour on the screen and one recorded in a colour atlas produced on their own particular colour printer. Perhaps the most important tool in the computerized design studio is the colour printer. A wide selection of devices are available using a variety of technologies – from ink jet through thermal wax to dye sublimation. A whole range of colour copiers have computer interfaces allowing them to be used as both printer and scanner in addition to their primary function. It is becoming increasingly difficult to tell the difference between computer-generated artwork and handmade. Printers have improved dramatically in quality over the last five years and they have gone down in price. They now accommodate a variety of media so that photographic quality images can be produced in magazine format, logos can be printed on to acetate and labels and all-over designs can even be printed directly on to fabric. Each printer, however, has its own colour spectrum – some are better on bright colours, others on pastels; none, as yet, can offer a full colour spectrum nor can they offer special effects like metallic or fluorescent dyes. CAD/CAM users have to be careful to select devices that meet their business needs.

The other obvious area where computer systems are scrutinized is in the field of screen resolution and colour fidelity. The fundamental limitation is in the technology of TV screens where light is emitted from the display and the colour we see is a mixture of red, green and blue phosphors. Almost all existing colour standards (Pantone, Scotdic and so forth) are defined with reference to paper or cloth, each using inks or dyes to produce colour that we perceive as absorbed or reflected light (none of them acts as a light emitter).

SAMPLING

Perhaps the most expensive process in any clothing company is that of sampling. A company will frequently have to produce designs in a variety of colour combinations and without CAD there is often the same labour content in creating the second version of a design as the first. Sample fabrics are also produced as a way of convincing the buyers of its look and feel. The greater the complexity of fabric production, the greater the cost of sampling both in time and in materials. For extremely complex fabrics such as lace it may take two weeks to set up a machine to produce a sample length of material and in consequence it is not unreasonable to produce only conservative designs that are highly likely to sell. The cost of a sample may be as much as £10 000. Even a relatively simple woven fabric sample can cost £2 500 when the entire cost of sampling is taken into account.

Consider the processes involved in selling a garment to Marks and Spencer: the idea has to be created, the first sketches produced, patterns generated, garments fitted, fabrics selected, colour chosen, trimmings sourced and so on. Each stage of this has to be 'sold', either internally or externally. For this process CAD systems that produce realistic output are seen to give significant benefits.

All systems now employ the same range of computer paintbox functions and images can be distorted, re-coloured, stretched, squashed, rotated and generally amended in a free manner. Many systems allow distorted fabrics to be superimposed on photographs so that images of real models wearing simulated garments can be produced. Material like this is often used to show ideas to clients before actual samples are manufactured.

Due to the ever-present demand for samples there has been a move towards the production of textile designs by directly printing on to cloth. Two manufacturers – Stork and Iris – have pioneered this technology and a few companies are using it to enhance their design studios. Coats Viyella has used the Stork technology to develop an understanding of the dyes used in the printing process to create colour-fast fabrics on a limited set of material types. Courtaulds uses the Iris printer, which at the time of writing does not give completely colour-fast fabrics but is quicker because it does not require a steam room to fix the dyes like the Coats Viyella system. The costs of these devices is still high (between £40 000 and £80 000) and the users have had to develop technical competence in their use but the effect on the link with the retailers is wonderful: the 'real' garments conveying far more than an image can, no matter how good the reproduction.

CAD itself does not appeal to all designers, some of them suggesting that it is sterile and lacks the depth of traditional media. Others complain about the unnatural nature of the computer tools or the difficult user interfaces. Most complaints are because comparisons are drawn with existing practices and once the initial resistance is overcome and users view the technology as a new set of media wonderful results can be expected. One company, Rosila, offers a complete CAD bureau service and it has experience in recruiting designers. About 60 per cent of its applicants find CAD easy to use and stimulating to the creative process, the other 40 per cent revert to traditional methods. Rosila has yet to find a formula to identify good potential users!

CAD in all fabric design is restricted to two-dimensional activity. Research work is slowly revealing the potential of 3D design, especially in knitted fabrics. The concept is of great interest to pattern technologists who love the idea of being able to design in three dimensions using ready formed items like shoulders and sleeves and so supplement the traditional methods of creating shape by joining two-dimensional curves. Chapter 8 contains more details about 3D design and the future of CAD/CAM.

TEXTILE MANUFACTURE

The process of turning a design on paper into a production fabric is always time-consuming. Printed textiles require colour separations – one for each colour in the final fabric. Woven fabrics need weaving plans showing yarns and lifting plans for the looms. Knitted fabrics require stitch detailing, structure and colour change information, and so the list goes on. A lot of labour is involved

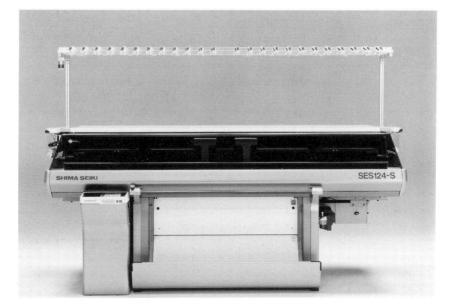

FIGURE 1a   Knitting machine SES 124-S
(Courtesy of Shima Seiki)

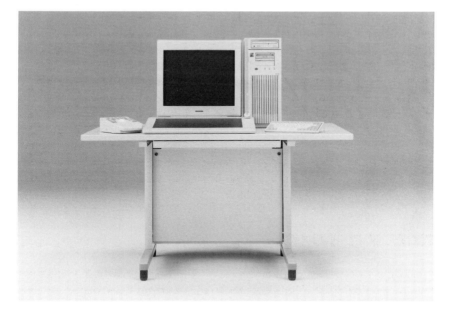

FIGURE 1b   Computer design station
(Courtesy of Shima Seiki)

in the process of converting paper designs into 'real textiles'. Naturally the benefits of the technology do not appeal only to the designers: it is in the transfer of data to the production process that great efficiency savings can be made and where CAM takes over from CAD. Printed textile designs can be transferred to laser engravers or can be output in colour separation form on acetate for use in the traditional printing process. Knitted fabrics are produced on machinery controlled by output direct from the CAD systems (Figure 1) and transfer of design to looms to weave materials is also electronic.

FABRIC MANUFACTURERS

There are three main types of fabric producers who can use CAD, namely those who produce knitted fabrics, those who make woven fabrics and those who create printed materials: each has specific requirements and systems are available for each part of the market. All three often use the same design software for the creation of the original ideas and the output is passed to the specialist packages for interpretation in the appropriate manner. Computer software for each creates repeat patterns so that users can see the effect of their work in the context of an overall pattern.

Details of suppliers of CAD/CAM systems for textiles applications can be found in Chapter 4.

YARN AND FIBRE PRODUCTION

The work undertaken by fibre suppliers is often very specialized and is not directly suited to CAD. There is, however, a great deal of work being undertaken in the promotion of yarns and fibres. Bodies like the International Wool Secretariat (IWS) use a variety of CAD/CAM systems to show potential customers the appearance of different colours and styles of yarn in a variety of woven or knitted products. The systems they use are primarily those geared to simulation and, in addition to showing the structure of the fabric, the colours and thickness of the yarns, they are able to simulate the structure of the yarn so that the effect of different twists can be viewed before sample making.

Another facet of the work undertaken is prediction of colours, styles and trends, and the main producers each have their own teams researching the market. Many of the original ideas come from this quarter and the companies use CAD/CAM technology to assist their design and promotional work. Catalogues are created using a variety of graphics systems and images are manipulated to convey both technical and aesthetic information. As new yarns become increasingly popular (was there a time before Lycra®?) and as the properties of man-made yarns are demanded by the public the value of the research and promotional work is realized.

Surprisingly there is little direct use of CAD/CAM systems as a means of supplying information from the yarn producer to the fabric manufacturers in electronic form. Although the capability exists there is often a great difference between the modelling work in the research laboratories of a yarn producer and that in the design studio of a fabric manufacturer. This difference centres largely on the need for accurate scientific data to simulate properties and the aesthetic considerations required by the fabric manufacturer. The next development in this area is to mix the two together so that fabric modelling can be based on the behavioural characteristics, structure and colour of the yarn(s) from which it is made, coupled with the structure of the material and the finishing process that creates the final product. It is only in areas like car seat design that the modelling work revolves around both scientific and aesthetic properties.

In addition to the main processes described above, specialist CAD/CAM systems are available for embroidery, for lace design and for appliqué work and other surface decoration. The first two are complex industries in their own right, each having specialist production machinery and each with its own specialist supplier base.

EMBROIDERY

Embroidery systems can take input from a range of graphics packages and then produce output on any size or scale. Like both woven and knitted products they have to work with a limited number of coloured threads but they also have to consider the total effect, making allowances for the stitch density and the substrate material. In fact the technical details of stitch processing are central to the functioning of any embroidery system.

Embroidery design systems tend to be linked directly to production equipment and their users usually make samples on small single-headed machines. There is less use of simulation by embroiderers than other CAD/CAM users, partly because embroidery provides a relief on top of a fabric, thereby giving it some three-dimensional properties.

Input to systems can be in the form of scanned images or by sketching ideas directly on to the computer screen. Stitch processing software is then used to fill in blocks of colour with different thread formations using both colour and structure to create the desired effect. The resulting data can be transferred electronically to the production machinery for manufacture.

LACE

Lace design is separate from production and the majority of production systems work by digitizing input on a large scale (about six times normal size) and then tracing the course each thread will take as it moves through a design. This, too, is a highly skilled and very complex process that takes significant time. Output is then via disk, tape, microchip or direct cable connection to the production machinery.

Lace is a complex structure, essentially mixing the knitting and weaving processes. The use of CAD to create original ideas has taken off in the 1990s and has been used to release the talents of designers on new concepts. Previously designers were unable to simulate a piece of lace since the time taken to create a manual illustration could not be justified – indeed it would require a high calibre artist – and so illustrations were necessarily simplistic and showed detail in small sections only. Samples made on production machinery were the means by which concepts were sold. CAD systems now produce incredibly realistic output which is often of sufficient quality for buying decisions to be made. As yet there is no direct link between the design system and that used for production: the threading process is so complicated that no automatic process yet exists. It is only a matter of time!

In all the above cases output from the CAD process is generally on to paper. There is one ecological advantage of the technology: rejected ideas no longer consume materials as users are able to make decisions on the screen before prints are made and so minimize waste. Considerable expense is also saved on media: pens, crayons, paints and inks often dry up before they are finished and as colours come in and out of season it is necessary to have a comprehensive set of each.

Output is also available in electronic form ready for transfer (where appropriate) to the production process – essentially when CAM begins.

CLOTHING

To appreciate the ways in which garments are made it is important to have an insight into the thought processes in clothing companies. Most businesses keep standard templates of shapes (known as 'blocks') that are used as the basis for the majority of their patterns. These blocks are traced on to pattern paper and modifications are made according to styling details. Rarely are dramatic changes required, most clothing being fairly conservative. It is only a change from highly tailored to looser fitting garments that requires the derivation of new blocks. In most clothing companies the use of patterns is essentially a 2D operation, samples being made to identify problems in fit and form. Some companies even unpick existing garments, sourced from around the world, to derive new pattern blocks from which copies and derivatives will be made.

2D VERSUS 3D

The art of the pattern cutter is in wrapping the 3D human form in materials that are cut from 2D fabric. Many of the top fashion designers achieve their creations by draping fabric on to a dress stand and pinning, cutting and shaping according to their creative instinct. To them a pattern is dynamic, evolving with their design, the final templates being taken by unwrapping the model and laying the fabrics on to paper for tracing out.

The diversity of the two starting points – one from a flat 2D pattern modified and joined together to form a 3D shape and the other from a 3D draping process – gives an indication of the problem facing the computer programmer entering this field. The couture houses have generally been opposed to the use of technology, feeling that it reduces the personalization of their creations, and the clothing companies have never demonstrated the need to manipulate patterns in 3D at the design stage. From both points of view one common theme emerges: understanding the human anatomy is the key to good pattern cutting. Understanding fabrics and drape is the key to aesthetically pleasing garments.

It was in the field of clothing that the first CAD/CAM systems were employed. They started with the process of marker making and have developed 'backwards' through grading to original pattern design. Almost all their function has been developed for flat patterns and they therefore work in two dimensions. Attempts at working in 3D have generally been abandoned due to the time-consuming and complex nature of making patterns in 3D.

The majority of clothing companies do not use CAD for original design work: systems are generally used for pattern engineering, grading (the construction of different sizes of garment) and lay planning (the creation of the cutting plan to minimize on cloth costs) and therefore are part of the manufacturing and production facilities rather than an integral part of design.

In many cases data is passed from the design room to the production facility in non-electronic form. Despite the wide availability of suitable systems it is rare to find a plant ready to use these facilities for original design. It is the lack of direct flow of construction data from design to production that causes a major bottleneck in many organizations: a re-engineering process is often undertaken as the means by which prototypes are turned into manufacturable items.

The following two sections explore the sequence of operation in a company, starting with pattern design and ending with garment production.

PATTERN INPUT

The most accepted method of inputting patterns to a CAD system is via a digitizing tablet (Figure 2). The method is simple: users tape their template on the surface of the tablet and identify key points to the computer using a 'puck'. By pressing one of the coded buttons they tell the system whether the point is the end of a straight line, part of a curve or a notch point. By this process information is entered and there are procedures to indicate the

FIGURE 2   Pattern digitizing (Courtesy of Gerber)

grain line of the pattern and other relevant data. Some systems do not require such a disciplined approach to pattern input and users can use a pen rather than a puck and create computer patterns using a blank piece of paper and their normal draughting tools (set squares, French curves and the like) – the digitizing tablet picks up their movements and translates them into an electronic pattern on screen. Other systems offer a pattern creation package whereby users input certain key dimensions and the system generates blocks according to the in-built rules. These rules or 'recipes' can be created by the individual user company but they will require some computer programming skills to capitalize on the idea.

PATTERN MODIFICATION

Once a company's complete set of pattern blocks has been entered into the system they are available 'on-line' for all successive users. The majority of systems offer the same functions for pattern manipulation – lengthening and shortening, cutting and combining pieces, adding pleats, folds and tucks, manipulating darts and so forth and are all commonplace.

Once a pattern is represented on screen there is a wealth of functions to facilitate the adaptation and modification process. These operations replace the traditional cutting, taping and tracing exercises performed on paper or

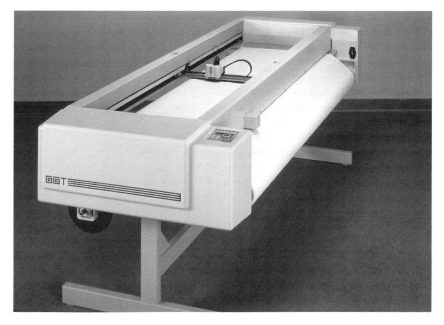

FIGURE 3   Pen plotter – Accuplot 320 (Courtesy of Gerber)

FIGURE 4   Sample cutter – DCS 500 (Courtesy of Gerber)

card and have the benefit of being commutable – something that has been changed can be restored to its original form instantly. Some CAD systems allow users to test 'sewability' by checking seam lengths and notch positions. Competent use of a CAD system will save time but is no replacement for good pattern cutting skills. Output of patterns is generally via a pen plotter (Figure 3) on to paper but there are a few sample cutters (Figure 4) that can cut card or even fabric and therefore speed up the process of sample making. Once pattern pieces have been entered into the system they are stored for re-use and modification whenever new designs are required as derivatives of older ones.

Some designers disliked the early systems as they operated in a very logical, mathematical manner and did not allow freehand curves to be drawn. The suppliers have made significant efforts in the last few years to make clothing systems more 'user friendly' by improving the digitizing process, enabling standard devices like set squares and French curves to be used during the digitizing process, and this is leading to more companies using the systems for original pattern design and modification as well as grading and lay planning.

GRADING

The great benefits of computers in saving time and improving accuracy become apparent in the grading process. Manual methods involve a combination of moving points, tracing shapes and checking seam lengths. It is a skilled process for the way in which seams are formed is critical to the look of the finished item and even a subtle change in the shape of a curve can have unacceptable consequences. CAD/CAM systems do not have any of the intelligence that can identify problems with shaping but they can generate the 'nests' of patterns in seconds and they offer tools for users to check lengths of seams and then make changes.

The systems require the user to tag certain points on the base size garment with 'grade rules' that indicate how each point moves across the different sizes. The computer system then generates the entire range of sizes by moving the points according to the movements specified in the individual rules and drawing in the new lines using the original shape as a guide (Figure 5). Users can check individual sizes and rules can be changed or adapted on an iterative basis to achieve better fit. Although conceptually a simple process, the knowledge of the human form in 3D and its relationship to the 2D pattern pieces is a prerequisite to good computerized grading.

In the grading process the effect of all systems is to produce nests of patterns according to the rules a user has associated with a base size. Systems differ in the level of intelligence they allow for the attachment of rules, for example a basic block may have rules to generate a complete set of sizes. These

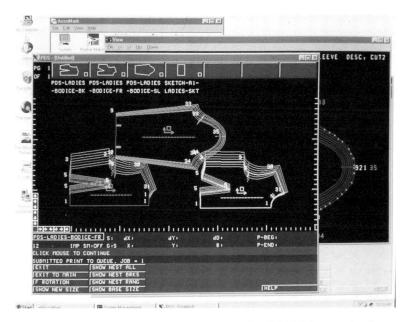

FIGURE 5   Graded nest – Accumark 100/200 graded
            pieces (Courtesy of Gerber)

rules would be attached to specific points on each block. When a pattern is
derived from this block it may involve significant adaptation and even splitting
the piece into two. Some CAD systems will automatically generate rules for
the new points while others will keep only the original information. Neither
is perfect as the exact nature of the user's adaptation may reflect non-linear
movement or could demand specific styling needs. Therefore both systems
need subsequent checking. Most systems allow users to measure individual
seams and therefore confirm the basic sewing lines of each size.

LAY PLANNING

Lay planning is always a critical part of any production company – it is vital
to cost and manufacture cannot begin until it has been performed and cutting can start. Consequently there is always a consideration between the
amount of time that can be devoted to the process and acceptable levels of
cloth use. A great advantage of a computer system is that cloth use is con-
stantly monitored and users have all the pieces at their fingertips on screen
(Figure 6). No longer do cardboard templates have to be traced on to paper
by hand. This alone saves significant time.

Many systems offer a 'quick and dirty' lay planning function (sometimes as
an automatic process) that allows the designer to estimate the amount of

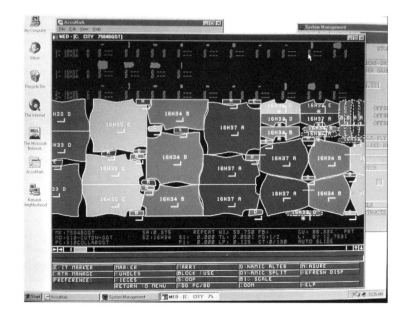

FIGURE 6   Lay plan – Accumark 100/200 marker making
(Courtesy of Gerber)

fabric a particular garment will consume, contributing to a preliminary cost-ing. This information often prompts the need for changes that will reduce the fabric requirements, sometimes with minimal change to the aesthetic qualities of a product. A good example would be in the creation of a circular skirt: by cutting in three panels rather than two it may be possible to pack pieces more tightly on the width of cloth available.

MARKER MAKING

CAD/CAM systems come into their own in the production environment when they are used to make markers as cutting plans. Whether or not the company has automatic cutting machinery the process of creating a marker involves a significant amount of human skill and experience. There have been many attempts at automatic marker making but as yet none is able to improve on an expert. The key to the success of computer systems is their ability to let users try out different combinations of packing by recording the efficiency at each stage. By this method good practice will soon indicate acceptable levels of waste and as the process is generally conducted at a single terminal the process occupies minimal space and takes significantly less time than purely manual methods (just walking up and down a table tracing pattern pieces on to paper involves time and effort).

The starting point for marker making is an indication of the quantities of each size of a garment that are required. This is then supplemented by details of the cloth to be used (notably its width and any surface or pattern details such as the width of a stripe or the density of a check), the number of pieces of cloth that can be cut simultaneously (the depth of the cut and the thickness of the cloth being used to determine this) and the maximum length that can be cut at any one time. Most systems will then divide the sizes across a series of markers and each will be laid out as an interactive process. For example, the first marker may contain three size 12s, two size 14s and a single size 16, the second may include two size 10s, one 16 and one 18. There is often good logic behind this division; sometimes by putting together a large and small size a better packing density can be achieved than by grouping similar sizes.

Once the ratio is established the process of packing all the pieces on to the cloth begins. Some systems offer an automatic procedure but none has yet to beat a human performing the same task. Primarily this is because an experienced operator will know when a piece can be rotated slightly off-grain with no impact on the finished goods or when a seam can be cut into the selvage. Instructing a computer how this can be done is not yet possible. However, an automatic process has the great advantage of producing an accurate indication of the maximum amount of fabric that will be needed for the manufacturing process and this can then be checked against stock levels. As users become more experienced, managers gain a feel for the general improvements that are achieved by the human operators. A rule of thumb develops along the lines of 'the automatic process says 450 metres, we know we normally improve on that by 3 per cent so we will reserve 436.5 metres'.

Output from marker making is generally performed via a pen plotter on to paper which can be used as a direct cutting template. Each piece is labelled with its name and size so that bundles can be assembled easily and efficiently after the cutting has taken place. A number of suppliers also offer automatic cutting machines and for these systems output additionally takes the form of a tape, disk or direct link to the machinery. Paper templates are generally still used to lay on top of the cloth (again for labelling purposes) but the cutting process is performed by machine rather than by hand (Figure 7).

Of course, the more advanced systems have direct links between the design, grading and marker making functions so that a design change can be made at any time, its impact automatically reflected through all the sizes and then on to the markers. Sometimes this works in reverse: a marker maker may identify a saving on fabric if a minor change is made to a pattern piece. CAD/CAM often acts as a two-way communication between designers and production staff.

Details of suppliers of CAD/CAM systems for clothing design, grading and marker making are provided in Chapter 4.

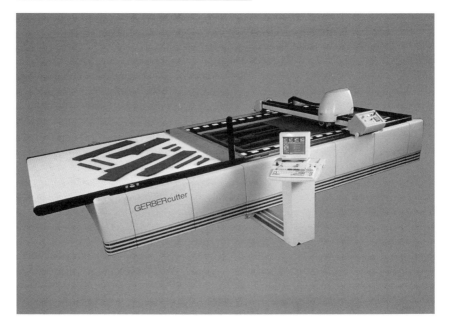

FIGURE 7   Cutting machine – S 5200 (Courtesy of Gerber)

EXPLOITING CAD/CAM FOR COMMUNICATION

Retailers use CAD primarily as a means of communication with their manufacturers and secondly with their stores. As many retailers employ a large number of manufacturers in locations all over the world they need to identify their requirements for design, assembly, sizes and packaging in a way that is easily understood. The use of CAD to illustrate ideas, to explain assembly instructions in diagrammatic form and to indicate how size charts should be applied is accepted practice and often helps communication with manufacturers whose first language is not English.

The need for co-operation between manufacturers and retailers is essential in any fast moving industry. For clothing and textiles companies the need for efficient communications reflects not only the size of the market but also the fickle nature of fashion trends and climate changes.

In the UK, unlike many European countries, a few large high street retailers dominate the market. Their adoption of CAD/CAM technology is the key factor in the growth of systems throughout the supply chain. Retailers use all forms of the technology with the notable limit on their need for actual production. Their use is generally geared to the relationship with their suppliers and customers.

There are obvious areas where CAD is important: it can be used to brief suppliers on new requirements for style, colour and presentation. It is used to plan the layout of shop floors and across the merchandising activity in everything from packaging to in-store display material. Retailers have to disseminate information such as size charts and basic block patterns to their manufacturers and CAD is one means of doing so. Manufacturers with CAD/CAM systems can receive the information electronically thereby saving time and avoiding transcription errors. There is an obvious need to ensure data is compatible: sometimes not a trivial process when the retailer's system comes from a different manufacturer.

The number of iterations between retailers and suppliers can be surprisingly high – even small changes require designs to be re-worked and frequently there is competition between manufacturers to meet deadlines and reflect buyers' wishes in their work. Often the reason for the number of changes is an inability to communicate effectively and this is where the greatest potential for interactive CAD occurs. Working via a telecommunications link it is possible for a designer and buyer to exchange ideas and refine details interactively, communicating style, colour and construction detail, and sharing information in pictorial form. Such communication offers enormous time savings and reduces the need for travel and face-to-face meetings.

Perhaps the most visual aspects of this type of computing come from the ability to create photographic montages from a variety of media: the ultimate in 'cut and paste'. Many low cost systems also provide the ability to change colour and texture, to distort, crop and otherwise disfigure images, and special effects such as viewing the result through a fish-eye lens, cracked ice or frosted glass are all now commonplace.

In addition to the delights of graphics packages there is a wealth of multimedia systems that let users put together slide shows that mix images, photographs, text, music, video clips and audio commentary. These are becomingly increasingly common at exhibitions and have the great advantage that changes can be made simply and with minimal cost. Frequently these types of systems are replacing the video tape as a means of presenting products to the market. Electronic catalogues now exist, both in the form of CDs and via pages on the Internet.

In terms of the relationship with suppliers there is a growing acceptance of design work that is presented as output from CAD. The links between buyers and manufacturers are based on a good understanding of each other's needs and, to reflect the ever-changing retail market, buyers often need to make last minute selections and to request design alterations. They realize that CAD is the means by which this can be achieved and they accept CAD output as an acceptable medium on which to make an initial buying decision as it will often precede a sample by a matter of days.

Another big task in any retail environment is to make the stores look as attractive as possible and to optimize the income that is derived from each square metre of floor space. CAD applications can contribute to this exercise. Architects have been using the technology for a long time and systems that can model building layouts in three dimensions are available 'off the shelf'. There are new developments to use these models as input to virtual reality so that users can see all round their stores to view goods on the shelves. Sainsburys has shown its initial ideas on television as a concept demonstrator of 'virtual shopping', the research work having been undertaken at Salford University. This experiment used photographic images as labels on boxes and cans to give some realism but all items were of rigid construction.

Clothing is, of course, flexible and to use the same concept for a virtual shop selling products that swing from hangers or are shown on mannequins requires significantly more work. However, the ideas are very useful and can be used in retail headquarters to give store designers an impression of layout and using VR they can wander about the store and see every angle from the shopper's viewpoint. This approach offers useful feedback when trying to see how a shop appears to a young child or someone in a wheelchair, as well as a 'typical' customer.

Packaging and labelling are very important to any store's image and retailers use CAD in all areas of this activity. Graphics work that would once have been contracted out now can be done in-house and ideas can be developed with the appropriate teams, passing ideas electronically between the participants. The output from each design team can be fed into the store model allowing ever more realism to be built into the concept. It can, of course, be passed in the same form to production houses or back to suppliers in a similar manner to ensure standards are met and consistency is achieved.

A new term, CSCW (standing for Computer Supported Collaborative Working), has been advanced by the Department of Trade and Industry. It aims to promote the idea of shared development and production work using computers linked by high grade telecommunications systems. A number of companies have already adopted CSCW principles without realizing the full impact of the technology. Primary applications have been built around shared data, both in terms of design (CAD/CAM) and production. Remote interaction between users has generally been limited by the availability of affordable broadband telecommunications and has generally been of a 'store and forward' nature.

Designing and communicating by computer becomes an ever more exciting process – capitalizing on new technology to gain a market lead remains the challenge for the clothing and textiles industry.

AN EXAMPLE OF DESIGN USING CAD/CAM

To appreciate the full impact of computer technology in the design room it is necessary to understand the work undertaken by a clothing designer. It divides into a number of logical parts: gathering ideas, translating ideas into illustrations, gaining approval from the potential customers for the concepts, performing the technical work involved in creating the pattern pieces that will be sewn together, developing sample garments, sourcing fabrics, yarns and trimmings and finally passing the finished product to the production process where multiple sizes will be created, matched to customer order requirements, and cloth usage optimized before the cutting and assembly process begins.

Many designers work in small companies, selling their ideas to larger groups for production. They often develop specialist skills in niche markets and exploit their talent and knowledge in highly creative ways. One such company is Katie McGuirk Associates, a specialist in children's clothing.

Katie determined her need for computer technology early in the 1990s and installed her CAD system in 1991. She invested about £25 000 in two systems, a scanner and printer, and had initially planned her use of the equipment as a 'scan in, make amendments and print out' process. In practice she has adopted a significantly different approach.

The first lesson Katie learned was that the CAD system could be used as a creative medium in its own right – the digitizing tablet and pen could be used as a drawing board and pencil. Once she had gained the necessary hand/eye co-ordination (a simple task) she found she could create her illustrations directly on the computer without the need for drawing on to paper and scanning the finished work. This saved time and (once she had organized her own internal computer filing system) allowed her to develop template shapes (characters, logos and garment outlines) that she could recall for other jobs. With this in mind she was able to share design ideas with her colleague.

With confidence in her own design ability, Katie used to print her illustrations, using the high quality colour printer supplied as part of the system. She would take these to her clients, knowing that she could produce multiple colour combinations and make amendments to the drawings without significant effort and without the need to start with a clean sheet of paper each time. The second lesson of the technology was that she became less precious about her work, knowing that it was the demands of her customers that dictated the success or failure of her designs, not the amount of effort that had gone into their creation.

As her clients became more interested in her work Katie realized that there was another way in which she could exploit the technology. It is often the case that clients request modifications or changes to her ideas requiring further work and follow up visits. Katie tried an experiment: instead of taking prints to her clients she took her computer. She now shows her ideas on screen and when changes are required she undertakes them immediately, developing a dialogue with the customer. This has proved to be enormously successful and is now part of her business strategy.

The third lesson of the technology has been the use of the psychology of the buying and selling process. By involving her clients in the final stages of the design Katie is able to gain their confidence, enthusiasm and commitment. Ideas are developed interactively and when she returns to her office she prints a copy of the agreed designs as confirmation of the customer's order. A natural by-product of this method is the minimization of waste materials: no longer are ideas translated on to paper simply for presentation and acceptance/rejection.

Possibly the next stage in Katie's work is to develop remote interfaces, using high grade telecommunications links to enable her to perform the same tasks but without the need for travel. Barriers to this idea are purely practical: each client will need suitable computer equipment and all parties will need broadband telecommunications links.

Benefits

O   Use of the technology as a creative tool
O   Less waste, lower media costs
O   More output and originality
O   Less 'precious' ownership of designs
O   More effective selling process
O   Greater understanding of clients' needs

PRODUCTION AND PROMOTION

Another company, Lindsay Allen Designs, in Scotland provides a further example of a CSCW user. The company specializes in high quality children's clothing sold through a series of agents. These people work on a 'party plan' principle, similar to the 'Tupperware parties' of the 1960s. They thrive on the originality and practicality of their designs, the quality of the product and the speed of delivery.

Kay Davidson-Taylor is the company's chief designer and she was a trial user of the Fashion Information System (FINS) multimedia database service (see page 113). FINS contains vast quantities of information in true multimedia format relevant to the industry. Core contents for Kay are the sourcing section (she has to buy large quantities of fabric and frequently needs to identify new trimmings and accessories like zips and buttons) and the forecasting agencies (she needs continual update on the directions for colour and shape being predicted by the experts).

Kay is an excellent example of a CSCW user, interacting with the database and extracting the information for use in other software packages (notably the design-oriented ones) that help her to develop ideas. She has learned how to manipulate fabric images and to superimpose them on photographs to make mock-up garments.

An experimental new facility has been added to the system, specifically for this company. An electronic catalogue has been created, its content being photographs and accompanying text relating to the current products in the range. Initially it is seen as a means of demonstrating the concepts of home shopping to the agents; its natural progression would be the provision of portable computers for each agent so that orders can be collected electronically and transmitted for each location back to the factory. Kay can obviously add her own data to the catalogue, opening new avenues for promotion and market research. As the company is highly flexible in its manufacture she can add her new designs to the catalogue (created by the process outlined above) before they have been manufactured, knowing the company can fulfil orders within days of receipt.

Benefits

O   New promotional opportunities
O   Easy sourcing of material
O   Direct links from electronic data to CAD process

These two small companies show how a new approach to the use of CAD/CAM can open new market opportunities, exploiting the technology as a medium by which business can be gained.

Some companies have made their name by offering CAD/CAM-based bureau services: they are all testament to the benefits of the technology and their capability spreads across the industry. There are those who specialize in grading, others in textile design while at least one company offers a computerized cutting facility. Some specialize in the more difficult challenges of design and others have a comprehensive understanding of colour. Although Coats Viyella has a complete computerized design facility for internal use it can also be used by others on a bureau basis. It offers textile design and sample production as well as pattern design and small scale production. A variety of CAD/CAM systems are used in the studio.

The larger companies are also the subject of media interest, though some prefer to keep their use of the technology to themselves. Some of the specialist techniques developed in-house to exploit CAD/CAM are used to gain competitive advantage and therefore remain confidential. As their own confidence grows and as the technology spreads there is an increasing realization that the technology itself is an insufficient competitive instrument: it is the use that talented designers make of it that determines commercial success.

INTEGRATED SYSTEMS

The larger CAD/CAM suppliers offer systems that integrate a number of functions. Elements like fabric selection, specification drawings and size charts are pulled together under the umbrella of a single database. Individual functions for design and production can still be performed but the great advantage of an integrated system is that different users can access the relevant data about a product, ensuring consistency of information and avoiding duplication of work.

These systems are best used in companies with a number of users, each with their own computer terminal, all connected via a network to a central storage device. Their full impact is realized when their operation fully complements existing work practice and individuals can add or extract data at any time during design or production. Some users have 'read only' links and cannot make changes to data while others have full access with the necessary authority to amend the contents.

These integrated packages allow the progress of product development and manufacture to be monitored more efficiently than by other means and therefore offer managers attractive benefits for ensuring efficient operation. They do, however, place an onus on business managers to ensure that all users maintain their data in an up-to-date, standard form so that information is both consistent and relevant.

Truly integrated systems are those that incorporate other aspects of an organization's work: sales order processing, stock control, payment and planning all need access to common data. There are very few companies that have yet implemented computers throughout their business. Chapter 7 takes a closer look at how CAD/CAD systems can be integrated with other business systems.

3

INVESTING IN CAD/CAM

❖

Any investment in CAD/CAM needs careful justification. This chapter aims to help company managers identify their own needs and educate themselves on the technology. It also offers guidance on the methods by which CAD/CAM can be integrated with existing work practices and therefore become part of an overall IT strategy, a point that is developed more fully in Chapter 7.

CAD/CAM is a very attractive technology and, as can be seen at the many exhibitions where it is shown, it appears to perform a large number of tasks efficiently and with great precision. Everyone will realize that the conditions at a show are significantly different from those in most studios or factories and therefore managers need to determine the justifications for its installation when performing 'real' work rather than providing demonstrations. There are no simple guidelines on the installation of a system but one observation is clear: an experienced user of a CAD/CAM system will be able to achieve more output in any given time than by using purely manual methods. (Readers will note that no comment is made about the quality of work produced – this still depends on the ability of the individual user.)

JUSTIFYING CAD/CAM

The majority of CAD users get hooked. Sometimes they wonder how they ever managed without the technology. The individual benefits differ widely between companies but most centre on opportunity creation rather than simple cost saving. Payback has been known to start within months of installation but there is no simple recipe for success. The value of a system is only realized in the hands of capable users and some installations lie idle in the corner of the design studio gathering dust because the magic mix of product and user was wrong.

CAM systems, too, generate an enthusiastic response when they have been implemented well. As they are generally more intrusive into a factory's operation their installation is often better planned than that of a straightforward CAD system. The cost of a CAM system is often high and therefore payback analysis is generally part of the sales justification process. A metric for measuring success can be set by monitoring throughput speed and volume, by minimizing cloth usage and by evening out the peaks and troughs of the traditional production environment.

In a well-integrated CAD/CAM installation the benefits of both systems are compounded and paybacks generally occur when the company can cope with increased demand both in quantity and variety terms.

The reasons why users believe in their investment can be summarized as follows:

- More innovation and greater consistency
- Quicker and more flexible response
- Enhanced quality of service and product to the customer
- Reduced operating cost
- Increased sales revenue
- Optimization of the spend on design and development
- Greatly improved communications
- Reduced sampling
- Creation of business opportunities and provision of service
- Contribution to business performance

The justification process itself is often more difficult than anticipated. Purchasing a CAD/CAM system always represents a significant investment and a simplistic argument linking cost to direct payback can fail. Some simple considerations may assist the decision-making process.

Cost justification in terms of direct payback is often difficult and managers should realize that the investment can often not be justified on what will be saved, instead it should be viewed on its ability to offer gains. Simple benefits like an increased throughput can be specified for processes like grading and marker making while less tangible metrics can be applied to creative designers using systems to support their development work.

The most obvious place to start any evaluation is by asking other companies what benefits they have gained from their investment and what problems they have encountered. Examples in Chapters 2 and 5 can be used as pointers; personal contact is even better. After looking at the benefits and pitfalls in a general manner the serious homework must start. This process must be geared to an individual company's own needs and will probably be carried out by the project champion. The guidelines that follow can serve as an action plan.

BEFORE YOU BUY

An observation made by companies that have successfully invested in the technology is the need to appoint a project champion, an individual who can be seen as the focus of the project, the driving spirit behind CAD/CAM, who is willing to get involved at every stage, from initial ideas through evaluation of needs, via specification writing to installation, training and exploitation. This person has to balance commercial pressures, technology capability and long-term corporate ambition and must therefore have the confidence of internal staff and managers.

The most important task for any project leader is to listen. This means taking advice from inside and outside the company and specifically demands that they gain a comprehensive understanding of user needs and capabilities and management's goals and aspirations. One document must emerge from the consultation phase, namely a *specification of requirements*. This is the primary guide for any supplier and for internal staff about the functions needed in the proposed system.

With this specification in place the shortlist of suitable software, hardware and suppliers can be drawn up. The information in Chapter 4 can be used to identify appropriate systems but some users will be able to purchase 'off-the-shelf' software packages to install on existing computers. This is especially true of applications that require predominantly graphics functions and text manipulation.

An awareness of the use that competitors make of CAD/CAM is very helpful and any knowledge that can be gained about their systems will be of value. It is, however, very important to acknowledge the fact that outsiders generally see only the results of using a system and rarely the methods that are employed to achieve them.

The most obvious suggestion is to identify a series of tasks that the company regards as suitable for implementation on CAD/CAM and to write these down as demonstration requirements. Distributed to each of the shortlisted companies, they can be used to determine the pros and cons of each individual system. This phase of a project is the *feasibility study* and is used to marry together ideas and capabilities.

It is important to involve internal staff in all demonstrations as they will be the ultimate users and their comments and suggestions will provide valuable feedback throughout the refinement process. During this period it will slowly become evident that some systems are more suitable than others and the shortlist should become a simple choice between no more than two or three systems. At this point the capabilities and functions may appear so similar that other determining factors need to be considered. Number one on this list is probably cost but really it should be personnel. The human element contributes significantly to the success of a CAD/CAM project and users should be able to identify which system seems easiest to operate and which seems most logical in its function. They will also have formed opinions about each supplier's staff and can offer suggestions as to which group seems easiest to work with.

One issue that may emerge during the demonstration period is the option to customize packages to individual needs. Many suppliers offer highly versatile software that can be presented in a form to suit a client's own mode of operation rather than imposing a rigid discipline from outside. The inherent flexibility of any system needs to be investigated fully during the evaluation period and staff must be prepared to challenge the suppliers to identify exactly how far a system can be pushed. The project manager must ensure that he or she fully understands what direct access users have to the data structure so that customization potential and data exchange can be investigated.

The final consideration that should inform the project leader is the future development plan – both the company's internal plans and those of the supplier. In the dynamic and competitive environment of the late twentieth century it is essential to identify a system that is flexible, upgradable and has the ability to exchange data with other packages. Most systems are provided in a modular form meaning that individual components (notably the central computer) can be upgraded without the need to replace other elements. Out of this phase of the study a single supplier should emerge.

Checklist

○   Identify the management's goals in its decision to purchase CAD/CAM
○   Identify the user capabilities and aspirations
○   Use these to generate a *specification of requirements*
○   Investigate the market fully before purchasing CAD/CAM
○   Take advice from colleagues and competitors – benefit from their experience
○   Produce a shortlist of suppliers that can meet the specification of requirements
○   Involve users and managers in the demonstration process
○   Understand the way that systems work – 'user friendliness' is essential
○   Ensure that data can be exchanged (imported from and exported to other systems)
○   Ensure that systems are upgradable in a modular form
○   All of these factors contribute to the *feasibility study* that will be used to select one supplier

MAKING THE PURCHASE

Provided the procedures outlined in the previous section have been adopted the serious negotiation can take place. Prices are always negotiable but there is no point in trying to install CAD/CAM on the cheap. The most expensive devices in any system are usually the colour printers and plotters and most suppliers buy from the same sources. Consequently the majority of price differential between systems rests on the cost of software, support and services. It is common sense to realize that the more of each that is required the greater the total cost will be.

The users will have been involved in the feasibility study and will usually be eager to get involved in the implementation phase. It is important to capitalize on internal interest and capabilities rather than employ specialist CAD personnel from outside. The primary reason for this is that the implementation phase demands that users identify how best to make the system work for their business and they will use all their knowledge and experience to ensure this happens. A new recruit may understand exactly how the CAD system operates but will not have the corporate knowledge that is the life blood of any company. It is advantageous, however, to appoint a manager of the system (probably the project champion) who has a good understanding of the technical elements of the system and of the company's products and practices.

During the installation and training period it is important to develop a strong working relationship with the supplier. As all the vendors are reasonably small companies it is beneficial to get to know staff on a first name basis. Much of the benefit gained from a close relationship is on the basis of informal chat and users will learn to understand not only how to use the product but also how others are getting results. This does not betray any confidences but simply exposes best practice and encourages competition. Unlike many other computer-based industries, a strong 'user group' culture where such information is exchanged on a more formal basis has not yet developed.

The final consideration during the implementation phase is for user companies to gain an increased understanding of the supplier's development plans. Much of this information may be informal but it can help users to identify opportunities to capitalize on new features as they emerge.

As well as learning about the system and the supplier internal work must be undertaken to capitalize on the technology. Like so many other aspects of the project the suggestions really amount to common sense but they are frequently overlooked in the eagerness to gain direct payback from the investment. Exploiting the system's potential needs time and lateral thinking and neither of these thrives in a pressured environment. Although the justification may have been made on a clear ability to deliver a few tasks, the full benefits will not be realized until users have developed their experience to a level where use of the system becomes second nature.

In many companies the greatest rewards from CAD/CAM have come not from the original tasks but from new methods of working that evolve during the normal operations. Designers in particular are employed for their creative talents and many therefore approach the technology with very open minds and investigative ideas. Sometimes they discover features that allow them to capitalize on their own talents and knowledge to create new ideas. They need time to experiment with the system without time pressures demanding instant results. In an ideal installation CAD/CAM will join other media in the design studio and will be used as yet another creative medium, complementing the human talent rather than threatening it. Remember, it is design skill that leads to success, not good technology!

CAD/CAM cannot be thought of as a 'one-off' investment. Companies must realize that computer developments occur incredibly fast and therefore new features emerge regularly. To capitalize on these and to retain competitiveness it is important to maintain a system in an up-to-date state and this demands regular investment. Sometimes a maintenance contract is sufficient, sometimes additional capital contribution is demanded.

Checklist

○   Develop a working relationship with the supplier
○   Train your existing personnel – do not employ anyone specially for CAD
○   Ensure that the system has a manager who understands both computers and clothing
○   System prices are usually negotiable!
○   Understand the supplier's development plans
○   Take time to learn the system properly
○   Let the system become an integral part of the design studio
○   Let users experiment
○   Keep the system up to date

AVOIDING PROBLEMS

Inevitably there will be problems with any system. Provided the procedures outlined in the earlier sections have been adopted these will be minimal in nature. If a purchasing decision has been made without reference to these recommendations it is possible that the chosen product will not be capable of performing all the functions required by the users. A system designed primarily for pattern grading and marker making cannot necessarily offer pattern design functions. Moreover, a good design system will not necessarily provide comprehensive marker manipulation capability. If problems of this magnitude manifest themselves then retrospective action must take place.

As it is unlikely that the system can be returned the specification of require-ments must be developed quickly and must be used to negotiate with the selected supplier changes to the hardware or software.

It will be the role of the project manager to ensure that realistic goals are established for the use of the system. Plans must reflect the time it takes for users to gain familiarity with the system and to become dextrous with the tools. They must also learn the discipline imposed by the system's filing structure so that data can easily be accessed and stored. For these reasons it is imperative that the CAD/CAM manager is competent, patient and an excellent communicator. He or she will have the task of setting goals and managing expectations within the company and will be the primary contact between user and supplier.

Often managers expect instant results and this has to be seen to be unrealis-tic. In many cases much of the initial work revolves around the transfer of exist-ing manual procedures into CAD/CAM terms. The input of patterns may take a couple of months and only when this is completed can managers expect 'instant access'. Since computer filing systems demand a disciplined approach much of the initial work requires project leaders to impose a naming and filing conven-tion appropriate to the company's other systems and compatible with the CAD/CAM system's own functionality. This task alone demands a sound under-standing of the technology and of the normal working practice and it should be performed carefully and critically. It must not be rushed. Sometimes the adop-tion of a standard approach requires changes to be made in other areas and therefore the installation of CAD/CAM can have far-reaching effects, often not recognized before the system is installed but essential to its efficient operation.

Problems will occur if the specification of requirements was incomplete or the system selected failed to meet its expectations. Other problems arise when managers' expectations exceed the ability of the system or the staff to deliver results.

Checklist

○ Know your system
○ Know your supplier
○ Know your media
○ Know your product
○ Plan realistically
○ Don't rely on CAD/CAM too soon after installation
○ Manage expectations

ADDRESSING DIFFICULTIES

Of course, if a company has done all its homework properly there should be minimal problems with any installation. Nevertheless it is highly unlikely that a CAD/CAM installation will be trouble free and difficulties need to be addressed up front.

If a system fails to perform according to the supplier's promise there are grounds for complaint. Identifying problems can be a lengthy process and this is when a good maintenance and support agreement is required. In many cases the difficulties arise from the 'real' work rather than that performed during the feasibility study. Simple things like pen plotters running out of ink, colour printers limited to ten prints per hour or pattern scanners that fail to identify notches correctly are all points that should have been discovered during the earlier phases but are frequently overlooked. Difficulties of this type must be addressed by reference to the contract between supplier and customer: if a system fails to meet its specified performance then there is a good case for redress. If problems are caused by faulty media (e.g. plotter paper was of an insufficient quality for the speed of throughput) then this too can be directed to the supplier.

There is an increasing need to produce output from CAD/CAM systems in electronic form for input to other systems and processes and consequently there is a trend towards the adoption of standards for data transfer. Patterns can be exported in a form that adheres to the AAMA (American Apparel Manufacturers Association) convention; images can be saved in a variety of formats such as TIFF, JPEG or BMP. The names may be unfamiliar to most users but they are independently documented and any supplier offering an 'open' system should identify exactly which standards are offered by its system. Some of the reasons for adopting standard formats relate to the needs of existing computer systems. Many have limitations on the ways in which they can accept or generate data and companies wishing to integrate CAD/CAM with other systems and processes must ensure compatibility.

Most difficulties arise from wrong use of the system, misdirected management or false expectations. In some cases this is because the project manager is unable to perform his or her function correctly. Sometimes individuals are appointed because they give the impression of competence but they lack a comprehensive understanding of the product. Jargon is frequently used to convey a familiarity with the technology but fails to interpret the terms correctly. This is a difficult management problem and is likely to involve discussion with the individual concerned as well as advice from the supplier. It may be that the company has been 'sold' a system rather than having made an informed buying decision and this is when external, impartial advice from consultants may be the only solution. They too need the specification of requirements as their starting point.

Checklist

O   Ensure that managers (especially the project champion) are technically competent

○   Use the specification of requirements as the definitive document to determine the fitness of purpose of any system
○   Ensure that standards are properly implemented
○   Ensure that suppliers offer products that meet their own specifications
○   Use independent consultants to address difficulties where direct dialogue cannot help

A DO-IT-YOURSELF CONSULTANCY GUIDE

Many companies employ consultants to help them determine which system to buy. Consultants are not cheap and before they can make recommendations they need to gain a significant understanding of their client's business. Much of their groundwork can be performed internally, assisting the selection process and reducing cost. To minimize the cost and maximize the impact of any consultant's contribution the following guide can be used by in-house staff to provide much of the routine data extracted during visits.

A commentary is provided at the start of each section to explain the logic behind the questions a consultant will ask. Some sections apply only to garment producers, others to textiles companies and so common sense should be used when attempting to use the guide in a self-help manner.

COMPANY DETAILS

The company needs to help a consultant understand its business, to identify the type of customers to whom it sells (e.g. a small number of large retailers), its trading history (e.g. has the company previously operated by direct selling), any specific strengths (e.g. was it the first user of microfibres in the manufacture of jackets) or weaknesses (e.g. attempts to sell to the teenage market were unsuccessful) and as much information as possible about the reasons why it is looking to invest in CAD/CAM.

By identifying contact personnel the company is starting to appoint project staff: individuals who will accept 'ownership' of the project and who will act as a primary liaison with the supplier and with internal staff. The observer will also note any political pressures for or against the technology, sometimes recognizing the divisions that exist right up to board level. This knowledge will help in the communication exercises necessary to demonstrate benefits: cynical views can often be used very constructively, particularly if they make all parties better clarify their justification for investment.

A consultant will make sure he or she visits the company on days when typical work is being progressed: any observations based on loading during slack times or peak production days need to be put in context of what is 'ordinary'. Observations about the proposed location of a system will help to inform the decision-making process about special lighting, air conditioning and cabling needs. The primary details they will note are as follows:

O   Address, telephone and fax
O   Staff contacts
O   Company history
O   Staff structure
O   Nature of company's business (products and services)
O   Major clients
O   Factory and office layout
O   Date(s) and day(s) of the week when visits were made

STAFF

The human resource is the most important part of most companies and without a clear understanding of the staff structure, the ways in which work is allocated and the particular specialist skills within an organization, it is impossible to recommend suitable IT systems to complement this resource. As the installation of a CAD/CAM system as part of an overall IT strategy has a potentially vast impact on staff roles and responsibilities it is very important for a project leader to understand the internal forces, goals and aspirations of all the workforce from the chairperson downwards.

As the CAD/CAM project progresses and installation is made it is inevitable that some jobs will change to accommodate the technology. These changes need to be specified in management plans and personnel should have the opportunity to capitalize on any new functions offered by the technology. Roles and responsibilities need re-definition once the technology is proven.

O   How many staff?
O   What are their names?
O   What are their roles?
O   What are their specialities?
O   Has anyone CAD/CAM experience?
O   Who are the managers and how is their reporting structure operated?
O   Who has been/is likely to be nominated as the project champion?

THE WORKLOAD

By identifying existing practices consultants can recommend transition strategies and naming conventions that will be sympathetic to the user community whilst maximizing the potential of a computer database. Sometimes issues like the monitoring and maintenance of quality standards become important (particularly in companies registered for ISO 9000). The introduction of a CAD/CAM package as an integral part of such a monitoring system can be an important contribution to management requirements. Similarly the ability to track work around a factory, from the original design concept to the dispatch bay, can help managers to monitor progress and report back to their clients, thereby creating a reputation for accurate, reliable delivery deadlines. All of these issues contribute to the consultant's assessment of the type of system, software and training needs.

From the design room onwards the flow of work through the company needs to be understood. While a CAD/CAM system may help to overcome bottlenecks it is unlikely to solve existing logistical problems. The patterns of work flow will determine the amount of equipment that is needed and a sound understanding of the workload will be advantageous when assessing training needs.

O   How is work fed into the design room?
O   Who directs this process?
O   How is the loading established?
O   Is it seasonal?
O   If so, how is it regulated?
O   What volume of product is designed each month?
O   How much variety is produced each month?

THE CLOTHING DESIGN PROCESS

The methods by which garments are created are central to the decision on the type of equipment that is provided. If a company generally starts its design work by tracing round block patterns and manipulating the shapes in an iterative cut and fit process a CAD system with an in-built library may be suitable. If the starting point is copying other garments then a digitizing facility will be needed. Decisions such as whether to work with or without seam allowances on patterns also determine what software functions are required. The checklist below covers the operations of a clothing company.

O   How are garments designed – from scratch? by modification?
O   How are specifications received and interpreted?
O   How is good fit ensured?
O   Are patterns created with or without seam allowance?
O   How is cloth sourced?
O   How are trims and accessories sourced?
O   Do designers perform costing exercises?
O   Who creates the markers?

CAD/CAM systems offer great opportunities for a company to organize its patterns more efficiently than is possible by manual methods. Clothing companies need to address these questions:

○   How are existing patterns stored?
○   How is the filing system organized?
○   How easy is it to access a specific pattern?
○   From where do the instructions for new patterns originate?
○   How is accurate fit achieved?

THE TEXTILE DESIGN PROCESS

In a textile company a similar list can be used, the questions this time relating to the method by which new designs are created (in-house or bought in from outside?), how much modification takes place and the methods by which samples are created.

○   Where are textile ideas sourced?
○   What level of modification and adaptation is performed in-house?
○   How are different fabrics handled?
○   What sample making facilities exist?
○   How are designs sold?

Other questions to consider include:

○   How are designs categorized and labelled?
○   How is colour controlled?
○   Who provides the link between design and production?
○   How do designers research their market and gain inspiration?

Both clothing and textile design studios will be asked questions relating to their specialist skills and to their market driving forces.

○   Who are the major competitors?
○   Does the company have any special design skills that set it apart from others?
○   What time pressures are there on the designers?

They also have a common set of organizational issues to address:

○   How are changes authorized?
○   How is confidentiality maintained?
○   How are design room problems identified and resolved?
○   How much interaction with the customer occurs in the design room?
○   How important is quality and delivery deadline to the company?
○   Do either of these areas currently need improving and how can changes in the design room help?

CLOTHING MANUFACTURE

Grading

A good understanding of the company's use of size charts will help to determine the grading functions required and the need to work to tight deadlines
will indicate the total time saving justification of a system. As grading by hand
is labour intensive the introduction of CAD will often save staff time and free
them up for other functions. Grading is frequently performed immediately
prior to marker making and this often means there is pressure on the grad-
er to produce output in very short timescales. CAD enables this to be done
but sufficient time for checking the results must always be allowed.

Since so much grading work is dictated by the retailers it is imperative to
assess the ways in which size charts are used and interpreted: significant
time will need to be devoted to the creation of grade rule libraries for the
variety of patterns and customers that characterize a company's work. The
suitability of a CAD/CAM system will be judged partly on its ability to cope
with the variety of grading tasks with which it will be presented.

- How are size charts used?
- Are there different charts for different customers?
- How many sizes are there in a typical range?
- How many sizes are there at most?
- Who does the grading?
- Who checks the results?
- How much time does grading take up?
- Is this always (often) on the critical path?
- Do the grading personnel have other skills that are of greater value
  to the company?

Marker making

A good overview of the current methods for creating markers and monitoring efficiency is essential. Most CAD systems offer marker making facilities but not all can cater for stripes or checks. Some are more automated
than others and all will be limited by the methods by which markers are
transferred to the shop floor for cutting. The exact nature of the marker
making process will vary between companies, especially when there is a
separation between the work of the design room (where the final function
is grading) and the production floor (which starts with marker making).
Companies will always strive to minimize waste fabric but without
CAD/CAM it is unlikely that they have ever had an accurate assessment of
it. All marker making systems record the efficiency (ratio between used and
unused fabric) and therefore minimum acceptable standards can be established. This sometimes means that design changes are required and so the

methods by which design changes can be requested by production personnel must be explained.

- How is material cut?
- Who makes the markers?
- How are patterned fabrics dealt with?
- How is efficiency measured?
- Are special limitations on markers posed by the nature of the company's work?
- How is a marker transferred to the shop floor?
- Who checks a marker?
- How much time does marker making take up?
- Is this always (often) on the critical path?
- Do the marker making personnel have other skills that are of greater value to the company?
- How are design modification requests from production dealt with?

TEXTILE MANUFACTURE

The first consideration in any company is the range of manufacturing machinery and the methods for its control. Many machines will have dedicated computer control mechanisms and therefore have predetermined limitations on the type of interface that can be provided from CAD. Sometimes the machinery is so tied up with production that it is impossible to use it to create samples and an 'off-line' creation of the machine control instructions, which may have to be performed outside normal working hours, is necessary.

Knitting

The transfer of a design idea to a production knitted fabric demands a knowledgeable translation from concept to reality. This is frequently achieved by the interaction between the designer and the knitting technician who tempers the ideas with the practical limitations of the knitting machinery's capabilities.

Output from the process is usually in the form of a floppy disk that is fed into the production machinery for mass manufacture.

Print

The majority of CAD systems allow totally free design functions to the user. The process of translation to production machinery requires practical decisions to be made. These relate primarily to the printing process itself: the number of colours to be used and the actual method of transfer on to fabric. Each method requires colours to be separated into unique combinations: a four-colour process will demand that each element of the design is separated into one of four primary colours (cyan, yellow, magenta or black) while a full colour process will require individual dyes to be identified.

Some printing machinery allows direct connection to the computer: ink jet printers are the obvious examples. Other processes require the creation of individual screens for each colour – the screens being created by laser engraving (a direct output from the computer) or by photographic masks, negatives being output from the computer in the form of printed images on acetate.

Weaving

Many modern looms are electronically controlled. Systems for the manufacture of different structures of woven fabric are readily available. Designs can be transferred to manufacture in a variety of ways, including paper prints. However, since most design systems for woven fabrics have direct output to specific weaving machinery it is usually possible to design and produce machine control instructions on one computer.

As with knitting, output from the production design process is usually in the form of magnetic media (disk or tape) that is fed into the manufacturing machines on the factory floor.

Embroidery

Embroidery machines are frequently computer controlled: designs are built up in layers from a combination of coloured threads. The design of an embroidered motif is limited by the size of the final design and by the quality of the product being manufactured. Designers can create any ideas but they have to be tempered by practical production and economic limitations. The majority of CAD designs systems for embroidery have different options for stitch formation allowing a variety of quality and density choices to cater for individual needs.

Like knitting and weaving systems, magnetic media is frequently used to transfer ideas to production machinery.

Lace

Although many modern lace making machines are computer controlled there is currently no direct link from CAD to CAM for lace production. This means that the input to the lace manufacturing process is normally in hard copy (paper) form, either as output from a CAD system or from manual draughting.

Lace production machinery requires specialist control instructions and the translation from a design to a set of machine codes involves knowledgeable staff in a detailed analysis process.

- How are designs transferred to production?
- What variety of machinery exists in production?
- How long does it take to set up each machine?
- Who controls the machine room throughput?
- How is productivity measured?
- How is quality monitored and maintained?

THE POTENTIAL OF CAD/CAM

So many opportunities open up when CAD/CAM is installed that companies often fail to capitalize on them all. A good consultant will look at these opportunities and recommend which areas can best benefit from the new technology. One implicit task in most consultancy jobs is to assist businesses to become more competitive and to gain a swift return from their investment. Many questions arise from the need to integrate CAD/CAM with other processes (see Chapters 7 and 8) and so a consultant will try to establish what other computer systems exist and what data transfer may be possible. The questions listed below are all geared to the speedy, effective introduction of the technology.

- Has the company used CAD/CAM systems before: either in-house or via a bureau?
- If so, when was this and what were the benefits and problems?
- What areas does the company identify as suitable for CAD/CAM applications?
- What CAD/CAM systems has the company identified as being suitable?
- Have competitor companies used CAD/CAM successfully?
- If so, who are they?
- What fears exist in the company for the introduction of CAD/CAM?
- Would staff feel threatened by the introduction of CAD/CAM?
- Would CAD/CAM be used to expand the company's business?
- What other competitive companies have been identified as benefiting from CAD/CAM?
- Does the company want publicity if it implements CAD/CAM?
- Does the company use EDI or have plans to use it?
- What other computer systems are used in the company?
- What data could be exchanged between these systems and CAD/CAM and in what format would it be most useful?
- Is the company driven by customer demands?

4

CAD/CAM SUPPLIERS

❖

There is a bewildering array of suppliers to the clothing and textiles industry. For even the most experienced CAD/CAM user the differences between systems are often difficult to determine and this means the selection process is increasingly difficult. This chapter aims to help customers to compile a short-list of suitable suppliers and to discuss some of the differentiating points between CAD/CAM packages.

Readers should appreciate that technology changes fast and new features are continually being added to CAD/CAM systems. Individual suppliers compete with each other for innovation and therefore it is impossible to provide a definitive guide for all potential users. It is worth noting that less than 20 per cent of companies have installed CAD/CAM systems and suppliers are competing fiercely for the remaining 80 per cent.

THE VARIETY OF SYSTEMS AND SUPPLIERS

There are over twenty suppliers of CAD/CAM systems, each offering a variety of packages suitable for use in different parts of the clothing and textiles industry. Each has prices based on hardware and software components, installation, training and support needs. Differences between systems are becoming less obvious than in the past and therefore customers have to gain a better understanding of individual functions before making buying decisions.

Some suppliers (notably Gerber and Lectra) have been around for many years and their internal expertise has been built around pattern cutting applications. Others are relative newcomers and have built their products around an understanding of modern computer systems and current market needs. In recent years all the pattern cutting suppliers have added presentation graphics to their product lists and some have entered the field of textile design. There is a prevailing trend towards more flexible systems that can interact with other packages and this in turn has led to an increase in competition and a decrease in price.

A feature of the CAD systems of the 1990s is the extension of their function to incorporate links to other systems and software packages. Products like PDM from Gerber accept input from a variety of sources and collate them together in the presentation of integrated specifications. These sources include design packages like Micrographix Designer, Fractal Painter and Photoshop as well as textual and numeric data and pattern specifications. Umbrella titles like 'Gerbersuite' are used to identify systems that incorporate a variety of software packages.

One of the driving forces behind these offerings is a realization that CAD has to extend beyond the design room and into the rest of the business, covering all aspects of clothing design, production, sales and marketing.

Because of the extensive choice it is almost impossible to make recommendations of appropriate systems to the general market and companies will need to identify their own requirements using the criteria listed in Chapter 3. There are, however, many common features that may restrict the options available. These include the type of hardware and software: systems may need to be compatible with other computer packages in the company or in its customers and suppliers. It may also be necessary for certain peripheral items to be provided (e.g. a device to print directly on to cloth or to produce knitting machinery control disks). The following sections can be used as a guide to the selections of hardware and software provided by the main suppliers.

Table 3 at the end of this chapter acts as a 'quick finder' to systems and suppliers but should be used with caution. All potential customers should develop their own assessment criteria based on individual needs: the table can be used to create a shortlist but not to make the complete selection.

HARDWARE PLATFORMS

There are three general types of computers in CAD/CAM systems: the IBM PC, the Apple Macintosh and Unix machines like those from Silicon Graphics and Hewlett-Packard. Each manufacturer offers at least one of these and the choice is shown in Table 1. By far the most popular machine type at the time of writing is the IBM PC.

One or two companies manufacture their own hardware as well as software. Lectra used to adopt this philosophy but changed tack in the mid-1990s to use industry standard products on both the Windows and Unix platforms. The knitting industry supplier Shima Seiki from Japan still supplies its own hardware and software and therefore interfacing to its systems from other packages is difficult.

TABLE 1   Computers and systems

Computer type	System (supplier)
IBM PC	PC Edit and PC Weave (Bonas)
	AJS Embroidery Services
	Compucon
	CAPT (Bracken Enterprises)
	Concept Design Studio (Concept II Research)
	CSB Meridian
	Cybrid PDS
	Eneas Designer (Cad for Cad)
	Gunold+Stickma
	Impact Pro (Eastman)
	Lectra
	Scotweave (Jeftex)
	Investronica (Macpherson)
	Nedgraphics
	Silhouette (Gerber)
	Tex-Data
	Wilcom
Apple Macintosh	Arizona (Bonas)
	AVA CAD/CAM
Silicon Graphics (UNIX)	U4iA (CDI)
	Stoll
IBM (UNIX)	U4iA (CDI)
Hewlett-Packard (UNIX)	Assyst

In this respect suppliers to the clothing and textiles industry are following the rest of the computer market, which relies on hardware from a limited range of manufacturers (IBM, Apple, Silicon Graphics, HP, Sun, etc.) or from the many suppliers of 'clones' (such as Compaq and Dell) who manufacture devices that function to the same specifications as those they imitate. The manufacture and support costs involved in the production of central computer hardware for specialist markets make it prohibitively expensive for most suppliers.

Although the computer hardware is the central element of any system, many different peripheral devices comprise a CAD/CAM system and many of these are identical on different configurations. In particular, colour printers and scanners are selected from the open market as are digitizing tablets and pen plotters. The range of devices for capturing and printing image data is extending fast: digital cameras give reasonable quality results while colour printers provide good colour rendition; both are inexpensive.

USER INTERFACES

The majority of systems use a 'point and click' user interface with instructions held in menus that are displayed on screen. Many suppliers have their own screen formats but there is a trend towards the use of Microsoft Windows layouts in packages from those companies using IBM PCs. Other interfaces include the use of menus printed on digitizing tablets while the older systems rely on users to type in commands via a keyboard.

Most systems supply a mouse as the primary input selection device but digitizing tablets with pens are becoming popular, especially in systems directed towards artistic applications where users are encouraged to draw straight on to the computer. One or two systems employ pens that draw straight on to the screen so that hand/eye co-ordination is simplified.

Another level to the user interface that is growing in importance as businesses become increasingly geared to electronic communication is the means by which systems are interfaced together. Some packages supply functions as 'menu items' that simply act as a method of starting one programme from within another. Others work on a 'multi-tasking' basis whereby two or more programmes can work in parallel with users switching between them using special keystrokes. In some cases the user interface in one application may be different from the others and this will require understanding on behalf of the user.

One of the main problems with systems that offer combinations of software from more than one source is the inconsistency between the terms that each employs. Trial and error are the only tools available to the user in the search for a common understanding. This trend will continue, especially as users demand more and more flexibility in their computer systems and require an increasing amount of compatibility and interoperation. No one supplier can offer the entire range of functions and therefore suppliers have to buy in that capability from outside. Unless they are influential enough to make their sources change terminology to match that employed in their own products the inconsistencies will remain.

The widespread adoption of the Microsoft Windows user interface is removing the main differences in appearance between packages (and is therefore removing some of the more obvious differentiating features between systems) but the internal functionality of each software module may be highly individual. This is obvious in the ways that big names in the market are being absorbed into other packages (e.g. the Corel Draw suppliers now offer Ventura Publisher as a desktop publishing package and although both use the Microsoft Windows interface they function very differently). As time passes and internal standards are adopted by all parties in an alliance so terms will gradually meld together into a cohesive set.

SOFTWARE

Software falls into two main categories – system software and user programs. The former is generally an integral part of the computer and is supplied by the manufacturer of that equipment. PCs normally use MS-DOS (Microsoft's Disk Operating System), supplemented in many cases by Windows. Larger machines may use UNIX (or one of its many variants like IRIX) or other proprietary packages. The suppliers of complete systems (e.g. CAD/CAM) and applications (e.g. stock control software) usually add their packages to the system by installing them on top of the operating system to perform the specialist functions. This means the basic functions (like recognizing input from a keyboard or mouse) are performed by the operating system and the specific functions (like grading a pattern or changing the colour of a yarn in a knitwear design) are provided by the application software.

SOFTWARE PACKAGES

The number of software packages in use in the industry grows daily, especially as the availability of inexpensive graphic design and image processing products on the open market means that competition is increasing choice and reducing price. To clothing and textiles companies this can be a headache since very few of these general purpose systems have all the facilities needed by the industry. For example, many of the highly productive design packages offer comprehensive 'paintbox' tools but do not have the ability to show images in the repeat form needed by textiles designers. To provide all the functions designers demand, a range of packages is required and this increases the cost and requires integration and training.

As products are tending towards the use of standard user interfaces the proliferation of software packages becomes less of a training problem and more one of cost and support. This tendency is also blurring the differences between systems designed for different hardware platforms and packages like Photoshop or Powerpoint are now available for both the Apple Mac and the IBM PC. Data can be exchanged between the two hardware platforms without conversion.

Some of the CAD/CAM suppliers include standard software packages in their own portfolio of software and this in turn gives inherent compatibility with other systems.

Table 2 links the different software packages with the system suppliers.

Most companies update their software regularly. Frequently the changes are based on feedback from users and it is therefore worth establishing the mechanics by which requests from customers are fed back to the development team. This is particularly applicable to British users as most software is written outside the UK.

TABLE 2   System functions and suppliers

Function	Systems/suppliers
Knitting systems	Shima Seiki ENEAS Designer (Cad for Cad) Stoll
Weaving systems	Bonas Tex-Data Scotweave/Jeftex
Printed textile design	AVA CAD/CAM ENEAS Designer (Cad for Cad) Concept Design Studio
Pattern design systems	Investronica/Macpherson Cybrid Assyst Lectra Gerber Concept Pattern Studio/Concept II Research Polygon/CAD for CAD
Grading systems	Investronica/Macpherson CAPT/Bracken Enterprises Concept Pattern Studio/Concept II Research Gerber Lectra Assyst
Marker making systems	Investronica/Macpherson Lectra Assyst Gerber
Embroidery systems	Wilcom Complan AJS Embroidery Services Gunold+Stickma
Cutting systems	Investronica/Macpherson Lectra Gerber
Integrated information systems	ProStyle/Lectra PDM/Gerber

INTEGRATION OF SYSTEMS AND PROCESSES

Perhaps the biggest challenge to CAD/CAM suppliers is to enable their systems to be used as tools in the integrated supply chain, using them as the means by which output is fed to the production and sales groups whilst information is taken as electronic input from suppliers and retailers. This demands a philosophy of 'open systems', a concept that is becoming increasingly more common.

The evolution of *de facto* standards for the storage of graphical images and the availability of inexpensive conversion software packages means that data can now be transferred between systems easily and accurately. Formats like JPEG, which is available on the Internet, are rapidly becoming the accepted standard for all CAD suppliers.

Attempts to standardize the format for storage of pattern data have been less successful with only one concept worthy of mention. This is the American Apparel Manufacturers Association (AAMA) file format that is based on a 2D draughting package (made primarily for the engineering industries) from the leading vendor, Autocad. The adoption of this standard is, however, problematic. Autocad was not written for the clothing and textiles industry and therefore does not include all the basic building blocks necessary to create patterns. Darts, pleats, notches, drill holes and the like are essential pattern items but they are transferred as discrete graphical items, not as integral parts of pattern pieces.

Curves do not always convert with 100 per cent accuracy and this is a notable problem when fitting two pattern pieces together. Grade rules attached to easily identified points are usually included without problem in any transfer but those along curves or part way along lines are not always represented. This type of standard represents the lowest common denominator between systems and therefore cannot guarantee comprehensive data transfer.

TRADE SHOWS, CONFERENCES AND EXHIBITIONS

To keep a watchful eye on the industry it is necessary to attend the many events that feature CAD/CAM. Three annual shows have become the leading events in the western world: 'Bobbin' in the USA is where most of the big companies exhibit their wares; 'ITMA' in Italy and 'IMB' in Germany are the two European equivalents.

UK events do not reach the same scale as these shows but are probably more useful to companies with the majority of their market in Europe. UK shows include 'Clotech' in Manchester and 'Computers in Clothing' in Harrogate. In addition, there are many events like the Textile Institute's 'Investing in Design by Computer' conference where systems are discussed and exhibited.

Sometimes the large events serve to confuse the visitor rather than clarify understanding of CAD/CAM. This is increasingly evident as so many software products are based on the same user interface. Shows should be used to gain a general overview of products, and will be the place where new developments are launched: anyone seriously interested in a product will need to follow it up at a later date.

BUREAUX, CONSULTANCIES AND COLLEGE RESOURCES

Some of the most objective advice and independent assessment of individual CAD/CAM systems comes from the various consultancy services that supply the industry. Many of these specialize on just one angle (e.g. grading services or cloth cutting) but they will have in-depth knowledge of this subject.

Colleges have the opposite viewpoint: they need to teach students skills that are required in the industry but try not to limit the knowledge they impart to just one package. All are working on limited budgets and therefore have to justify each purchase on its value to education and research. The practical experience gained in these establishments often helps visitors to understand the practical implications of training and this in turn can be used as part of a company's assessment of installation costs.

The creation of an individual company's own specification as outlined in Chapter 3 is essential and the resulting document can be used as the basis for discussion with any of the agencies. They will be able to identify many of the pitfalls and idiosyncrasies of their own systems and should be able to elaborate the reasons for their own purchasing decisions.

As many users of CAD/CAM gained their initial experience via bureau services there is a wealth of anecdotal data in these agencies that may help others to benefit from their competitors' experience. Bureau staff themselves are some of the most versatile CAD/CAM users. Since they derive their income from the provision of a service to a variety of clients they have to assess the right approach to each user's needs. As well as determining the right system to use they also have to estimate the time each task will take.

All suppliers have lists of their own customers. Some will be promoted as reference sites and every opportunity should be taken to follow up these contacts. Really successful users will be willing to share their experiences and can often guide a prospective customer in the right direction. Ideally they should be asked to comment on the suitability of the hardware and software for the tasks in hand, the value of the support they have received from the supplier, the reliability of the system, the time it took for users to become effective and its overall contribution to business success.

Some suppliers also run user groups. An aspiring client may ask to attend one of these meetings to assess both the value of the events and the issues being discussed. As such events also provide the opportunity to meet existing users and discuss their experiences of both product and service every effort should be made to attend them.

QUICK FINDER

In Table 3 companies are listed in alphabetical order. Telephone and fax numbers are given for each supplier. For callers outside the UK the leading '0' should be replaced by the international dialling code (44). Where companies have an e-mail address this is listed along with details of their World Wide Web site if appropriate.

TABLE 3   System suppliers

Company	Product(s)	Software
AJS Embroidery Services Limited Tel: 0115–945 9460 Fax: 0115–945 9229 E-mail: Info@ajs-embroidery.co.uk		
Assyst Tel: 01226–215060 Fax: 01226–215070 E-mail: INFO@assyst-intl.com WWW: http://www.assyst-intl.com	Assygraph Assyform Assycad/lay Assycut	Design Product data specification Grading and lay planning Cutting
AVA CAD/CAM Tel: 01625–506800 Fax: 01625–261378 E-mail: data@avacadcam.com.uk WWW: http://www.avacadcam.com		
Bonas Tel: 0191–491 0444 Fax: 0191–491 0999	Arizona PC Edit/PC Weave	Jacquard weaving design and loom control Weave pattern edit and loom control
Bracken Enterprises Tel: 0113–257 6545 Fax: 0113–244 8176	CAPT	Grading

Company	Product(s)	Software
CAD for CAD Tel: 0181–900 9240 Fax: 0181–900 9241	ENEAS Designer	Fashion design and colour simulation
	Polynest	Knitting design and stitch simulation Pattern design, grading and marker making
CDI Tel: 01926–431770 Fax: 01926–431880 E-mail; kevinmiller@cdi-u4ia.co.uk WWW:http://www.cdi-u4ia.com	U4iA	Design
Compucon Tel: 0115–949 9880		Embroidery punch and edit
Concept II Research Tel: 01438–313936 Fax: 01438–233122	Concept Pattern Studio	Pattern design, grading and marker making
	Concept Design Studio Drape	Printed textile design Garment sketching Pseudo 3D
CSB Meridian Tel: 0171–636 6178 Fax: 0171–636 6182 E-mail: london.csbm.prima@dial.pipex.com	PrimaVision	
Cybrid Tel: 01525–237203 Fax: 01525–377248 E-mail: jdp@cix.compulink.co.uk	Cybrid PDS	Pattern creation, grading and marker making Plotter/cutters
Eastman Tel: 01246–851576 Fax: 01246–855053 E-mail: SALES@EASTMAN.CO.UK	Impact Pro	Pattern design, grading and marker making

Company	Product(s)	Software
Gerber Garment Technology Tel: 0161–455 5900 Fax: 0161–455 5959 WWW: http://www.ggt.com	Silhouette Artworks Accumark PDM	Pattern design Pattern grading and marker making
Gunold+Stickma Tel: 0115–986 2561 Fax: 0115–986 2236 E-mail: sales@gs.uk.com WWW:http://www.gs.uk.com	Embroidery design/ edit and punch	
Jeftex Tel: 01706–372216 Fax: 01706–377305	Scotweave	Weaving design and simulation
Lectra Tel: 01274–580990 Fax: 01274–531119 E-mail: tmills@qm.lectra.fr WWW: http://www.lectra.com	Modaris Freeline Diamino ProStyle Graphic Instinct Style Manager Contour Vector Fly-pen	Pattern design and grading Pattern design system using drawing board digitizer Marker making Image manipulation Fabric simulation and drape system Concept design Product data management Sample cutting machine Cloth cutting machinery Pen plotter
Macpherson Tel: 0115–986 8701 Fax: 0115–986 4430 E-mail: 101500.2523@COMPUSERVE.COM	Investronica Microstitch	Pattern design, grading, marker making and cutting Embroidery

Company	Product(s)	Software
Monarch Tel: 0116–235 1502 Fax: 0116–236 7201		
Nedgraphics Tel: 0161–227 9937 Fax: 0161–226 5057		
Shima Seiki Tel: 0116–274 1515 Fax: 0116–274 1455	Total Knitting System	
	Total Design embroidery	Stitch processing, editing
Stoll Tel: 0116–253 8296 Fax: 0116–253 8219	Knitting	
Tex-Data Tel: 01773–880820 Fax: 01773–821284	Tex-Design	Sketching, illustration
	Tex-Check	Woven fabric simulation
	Tex-Dress	Drape simulation
Wilcom Tel: 0114–276 1244 Fax: 0114–276 1588 E-mail: sales@wilcom.demon.co.uk	Sirius Design	Embroidery punch and edit

5

THE TRUE COST OF CAD/CAM

❖

Investment in CAD/CAM starts well before purchase when the team first investigates the technology at shows, conferences and trade fairs. It goes on, usually over many months, while visits are made, demonstrations attended and specifications written. The far-sighted company will treat all of this activity as part of the training programme and will use the interaction with the suppliers as a means of acquiring the jargon of the market, and a familiarity with the hardware and software tools.

Payback is often expected immediately following installation of a CAD/CAM system but this is unlikely to be achieved: the best that a company can expect over the first six months is that users are able to achieve similar output to that attained with traditional methods. It is only when the system's tools are fully understood and when libraries of patterns, colours, grade rules and the like are entered that systems start to become really productive. In fact it is likely that productivity will dip immediately following installation as users take time to be trained and then practise their skills on the new technology.

The companies that benefit from CAD/CAM systems as soon as possible after installation are those that have done their homework. Ensuring that the chosen hardware and software will perform the whole range of tasks expected of it seems obvious but many purchasers fail to produce a full specification of their requirements and only discover a system's limitations after installation.

In this chapter some of the hidden costs are exposed and readers are given an insight into the implications of installing CAD/CAM based on the experience of others who have learned lessons the hard way.

MANAGING EXPECTATIONS

The cost of CAD/CAM is often confused with the capital expenditure on a system. This is a naive concept that should be rejected in favour of a more realistic view that takes into account the running costs, staff training time, support and maintenance. Although the capital outlay may seem to be the dominant figure, maintenance (usually in the order of 10 per cent of capital cost per annum) will figure significantly in an analysis of total costs over a five-year period. Media charges need to be recognized and compared with existing costs to identify savings or additional expense. Moreover, CAD/CAM is a greedy consumer of investment: as technology changes so new facilities become available and there is continual pressure to upgrade a system to capitalize on the latest features of both hardware and software.

Investment in CAD/CAM technology demands careful planning and this must be realistic enough to accommodate the decline in productivity in the first few weeks after installation. To ensure that the full benefits of the system can be realized users need sufficient time to familiarize themselves with the hardware and software and then become proficient in the skills necessary to operate the package. These skills will also incorporate a familiarity with the media, and experimental work must be undertaken to recognize both the potential and limitations of different types. The project manager must ensure that staff training and development activity is conducted professionally and with realistic expectations.

Managers often use the knowledge gained during the purchasing of CAD/CAM to extend their expectations of the technology and, introduced too early in the learning curve, these can be disastrous. Proficiency has to be earned and this takes time, frustration, dedication and talent. Targets for productivity improvement should be set only after a suitable induction period (at least one month) as additional pressure on users may lead to an extended learning curve. It may be that the system has been purchased because it is required by a retail customer as a means of transacting business: many companies specify EDI capability and there is a drive to use significantly more integrated systems, including CAD/CAM, for communication between parties. Sometimes it is worth informing large retail customers of the availability of CAD/CAM only once competence has been achieved.

Some companies are already CAD/CAM users and will be looking to re-invest: research work undertaken by Touche Ross in 1994 revealed that nearly half of those businesses with CAD/CAM facilities were looking to expand them. Problems are not just for newcomers to the field and companies often have to decide between investing in new hardware and/or software or extending their existing package. The choice is not always easy, especially as the underlying computer technology is moving forward so fast.

One option is for companies to lease rather than buy systems. The charges for leasing vary widely and not all suppliers offer the service. The benefit is simply that the user company is not tied to the initial investment and the depreciation of equipment does not appear on its accounts.

INITIAL CAPITAL OUTLAY

The amount of investment will depend on the facilities required by each user and the level of equipment that already exists. A few CAD users can purchase a software package for basic design work and spend no more than £200 or £300. They would install it on an existing computer (usually an Apple Mac or a PC), use a mouse for input and control, with a printer for output. Others may purchase a complete pattern making and cutting system costing over £100 000. Budgets will fall between these two extremes and with fierce competition between suppliers complete systems can be purchased for less than £25 000.

There are three components to the purchase of a CAD/CAM system – hardware, software and media – and the investment in each will depend largely on the supplier and the nature of the work to be undertaken. The easily identifiable parts are the hardware elements. The central item is always a computer and around this are hung a variety of peripheral devices (printers, plotters, digitizing tablets, scanners, etc.). The output devices (printers and plotters) are usually more expensive than those used for input. The software is the least tangible element and can be the most expensive component. It is, however, the most critical item and is often the main differentiation between systems. The final consideration is the media that will be used (e.g. plotter paper, knife blades for cutters and ink cartridges for printers). Although these do not involve a significant capital investment when compared with other components, they will contribute significantly to total running costs over a period of time.

The initial investment must not be viewed simply as the purchase of a collection of hardware and software. Instead CAD/CAM has to be viewed as a system and the initial outlay must include all the component parts, training, installation and ancillary costs. The total cost may appear prohibitive to many organizations but there is often an opportunity to phase investment, especially if the main expenditure comes from the provision of multiple user terminals. Managers must be aware that CAD/CAM is rarely a one-off investment and it is likely to demand continual resource over its full lifetime. In much the same way as the design of a company's products will change, so the function of a CAD/CAM system evolves and to capitalize on new features a company must have the correct hardware and software environment. Systems do, however, usually justify their cost and therefore companies will rarely wish to get off the technology bandwagon once the first installation is up and running.

Peripheral devices often dominate the capital cost of systems and therefore the selection of these devices has to be carefully tailored to user requirements. Of particular importance is the need to match the size of input and output devices to the work being undertaken: the larger the device, the more it will cost. For example, if a company manufactures only childrenswear it is unlikely to require the biggest size of digitizing tablet for inputting patterns. To assist in the assessment of quotations from different suppliers customers should request a detailed breakdown of costs so that the value of each item can be gauged.

INSTALLATION COSTS

A number of installation costs are associated with the arrival of CAD/CAM. Managers need to consider the implications of space requirements (and these must take into account the availability of adequate power sockets as well as lighting conditions), furniture and storage facilities. These all form part of the initial capital outlay.

To trivialize the need for planning at the installation stage is easy but the penalties paid by those who have failed to think through the operation should be taken as warnings by others. Apart from the obvious needs for each CAD/CAM user to have adequate space to work and for a terminal there is an essential requirement (backed up by European legislation) that demands that the ergonomics of the workplace are of an acceptable standard. This means that certain types of lighting are not permitted and chairs, monitors and keyboards must be adjustable to individual user needs.

Some organizations may not install a system on each user's own desk, preferring instead to run CAD/CAM as a central resource, with users booking sessions. The need for completely adjustable furniture and equipment layout is even more important in these circumstances: left- and right-handed users must be catered for as must the tilt of the monitor so that it aligns with each individual's eyes. Moreover, it is highly likely that different users will require different hardware and software settings and the need for a system manager becomes ever more evident.

Getting the cabling right is another important element of an initial installation, especially when a network is to be installed. Managers must decide on the type of network (e.g. is it a 'daisy chain' configuration or a 'star' system?) and the quality of cables that will be needed. They must determine the location of the sockets into which each machine will be plugged and may have to consider the need for specially screened cable, especially in factory sites where the operation of production machinery can cause electrical 'noise' which in turn will cause problems on the computer systems. Managers should also consider any expansion possibilities: with the correct grade of cabling it will be simple to integrate new facilities like video conferencing without disruption.

Obviously, reliable power supplies to the computer system, especially the central server on a network, must be considered. Uninterruptable power supplies come in many different forms but most operate only for a limited time period if the mains fail. Most systems with a central computer (file server) should be installed with uninterruptable, clean power supplies but most terminals can manage with ordinary electrical sockets. The location of all sockets must be close enough to each device to ensure cables do not trail over the floor and each device should plug into its own socket: adapters and extension leads should not be used.

Adherence to European legislation is not just a mandatory requirement, it is also common sense: much of the law has been set to ensure that problems with eyesight, backache or repetitive strain injury (RSI) are dealt with before they arise, and managers will realize that prevention is better than cure. Health and safety considerations are managed by sensible approaches to the location of devices and adherence to the basic legal guidelines.

The location of devices such as printers that may be shared between a number of users must reflect the work practice normally adopted: siting a colour printer in an office other than the design studio may result in many lost working hours while users trek to the machine simply to collect output. The geography of a site must consider the building infrastructure, the location of the users and the devices they require in their immediate vicinity.

ON-GOING SUPPORT

Perhaps the worst examples of CAD/CAM use are seen in companies that have failed to follow some of the simple guidelines for internal management and where on-going support and maintenance is not established. This is especially evident in companies where new additions have been made to systems without the supplier's knowledge or against their advice. For example, in one company a modem link from the CAD/CAM facility to another site appeared to stop working without reason. It took over a week to link the problem to the installation of a new telephone network in the building and in the end the cable was found to be of insufficient quality to transmit data. The supplier had been called to site two or three times and was able to state clearly that the fault did not lie with its equipment: every test it could apply was passed but the fault remained. Similarly the telephone supplier's kit passed all their tests. No one had told the cable installation gang that a modem was to be installed on one of the branches and therefore it was unable to foresee the need for superior quality cable. All in all this was a very costly exercise that could have been avoided by better internal management and technical knowledge of both the computers and telecommunications. This type of situation needs to be avoided as all parties can claim that problems are caused by equipment other than their own and resolution can only be achieved by independent arbitration.

Support is a much undervalued service. It should be used by the suppliers to inform customers of new developments as well as maintaining existing systems. All suppliers offer a variety of support contracts that cover hardware, software and telephone advice lines. Typical charges are based on 10–15 per cent of initial purchase price per annum and include regular maintenance of hardware, fault fixing, telephone support and software upgrading. Some users try and solve every problem by themselves while others are regularly on the phone to their supplier. The quality and cost of support varies considerably between suppliers, and purchasers should ask for references from existing users to evaluate the quality and value of the service. For example, one company with a CAD system has had such poor response from its supplier that the equipment lies unused in the corner of the studio because it is not capable of performing the task requested of it.

MAINTENANCE AND RUNNING COSTS

Running costs will vary depending on the type of CAD/CAM system installed. All systems consume electricity but none is likely to make a disproportionate demand on supplies. Running costs associated with a CAD/CAM systems environment should be determined at the initial planning stage. The replacement of mechanical parts and replenishment of media will incur the main running costs. Routine maintenance will be undertaken by internal staff and cleaning components, replacing media and calibrating devices will all be included in the training process. This maintenance will, however, take time and require skilled staff and therefore the cost of this must be taken into account.

MECHANICAL PARTS

All devices with moving parts will need maintenance and replacement of key components to keep them functioning at peak performance levels. Devices like pen plotters use a variety of mechanisms for feeding the paper and moving the drawing head. Any slack or wear in the mechanics will result in unreliable output – pattern pieces could be oversized or too small, lines may not join up correctly and breaks in the paper could occur. All plotter users therefore need to understand their devices and service them regularly.

Printers have the same limitations with moving parts and faults will occur with jammed paper, inks and thermal wax ribbons. Inevitably mechanical devices will go wrong and it is sensible for users to locate suitable repair sources and procedures at the time of installation. This means that companies will understand the potential costs and timescales involved in the repair of any component parts. Some may wish to opt for an on-site maintenance contract to guarantee continuity of service and ensure that disruption is minimized.

All devices need regular cleaning and servicing: ink jet printers are particularly prone to clogging if the print heads are not cleaned properly. Other printers are less problematic but all need their feed mechanisms kept clear to ensure correct functioning and paper alignment. Plotters, too, need their rollers cleaned to ensure that paper is fed evenly.

Companies that have invested in cutting machinery will recognize the need to replace knife blades regularly. Each different type has an estimated lifetime based on the depth and speed of cut linked to the types of materials being processed. In a company dealing with a variety of garments and fabrics no simple equation can be used to determine average lifetime of blades but experience suggests the cost can be significant.

Users should ensure that they fully understand the time it takes to repair any malfunctioning device. Once CAD/CAM is fully integrated into a company, production often depends on the availability of output from systems and if, for example, a plotter is out of action then markers cannot be produced.

All suppliers offer different grades of service for mechanical repair – typically within 4 hours, same day or 48-hour response. The charge varies significantly but is often based on a percentage of initial cost. Some suppliers charge for individual components including only labour in the service cost, others include full replacement of faulty parts.

MEDIA

Pattern designers require output in printed form. The usual device provided by suppliers is a pen plotter. All plotters require paper or cardboard and all require ink with which lines will be scribed on to the substrate. Pens come in a wide variety of types: from ink through roller ball to felt tip. Costs vary according to the type of device and the estimated lifetime. Ink pens are generally the most expensive types and felt tips the cheapest. Choice has to be made on both cost and quality of output required. Also the lifetime of a pen has to be considered: many users leave a number of marker plots to create overnight only to find rolls of blank paper the following morning where the ink ran out part way through the output process. Typical pen prices vary between £1 and £5 each.

Plotter paper is available in sheets or on rolls. The latter is usually cheaper than the former and frequently involves less waste. However, there is a tendency for rolls to be too thick for many plotters to handle (they cannot drag the weight of paper through the writing surface) and so shorter rolls are required. On other devices users may find that rolls that are not trimmed precisely at the edges have a tendency to wander slightly from side to side and therefore higher quality edges than the standard product are required. Paper is an expensive commodity and costs vary dramatically between different qualities – computer peripherals usually work better on the higher grades of paper and so charges are likely to be slightly more than the existing ones incurred for manual pattern cutting.

Textile designers also need hard copy output and printers require both the substrate surface (paper, card or acetate) and the transfer media (ink cartridges, thermal wax ribbons and so forth). Both can be expensive (costing up to £5 per sheet or £200 per roll). The variety of paper types suitable for use in printers is growing rapidly but the specific selection must be made to match the printer itself. Ink jet printers need paper of sufficient absorbency to accept the ink as it is sprayed on to the sheet but it must not be so absorbent that the ink spreads and the medium becomes unstable. Thermal wax printers use heat as the means by which wax is melted from the roll on to the surface of the paper and therefore the medium has to tolerate very high temperatures without burning.

Companies must ensure that they maintain adequate stocks of media to cope with demand, especially as some products (notably those that are available from only one or two sources) have extended delivery times from the manufacturers. Some media decays with age (pens have a tendency to dry up and paper stretches) so there is a balance between maintaining adequate stock and ensuring quality.

SYSTEM BACKUP

The process of system backup should be adopted as a normal part of any computer operator's life yet it is still one of the most easily forgotten tasks. Regular copies of the data should be taken for storage separately so that in the case of a system crash or an even worse disaster like a fire the company's key information (its designs) are safe and can easily be restored. In addition to the data backup it is sensible to take copies of the system software, especially any elements that have been added or modified for the particular client.

With older single terminal systems the process of backing up data means that the system cannot be used for its ordinary work during the backup. Depending on the age of the system, the quantity of data and the storage medium selected, this may take a few hours and may require an operator to control the process. Networked systems with a central file server can usually perform backups without interrupting the normal work except momentarily. The cost of backup must take into account the time taken out of production, the amount of staff involvement and the cost of the media. The cost of not doing so is potential disaster!

UPGRADING

CAD/CAM is not a one-off investment and provision should be made for regular updates and maintenance. Since surveys have found that the majority of existing users wish to extend their facilities there is justification for thinking that new users will follow the same pattern. Two driving forces lie behind the need to upgrade: one is the rate of change of the technology and the other is the ever-present threat of competition. Improvements in computer hardware performance occur at a remarkable pace: the speed at which computers function gets ever faster, the amount of memory they contain increases at a highly affordable rate, and devices like modems and CD-ROMs can be included in a configuration at minimal price. This means that any equipment bought this year may be considered out of date in twelve months' time. This view is sometimes used to delay investment but that is wrong. An 'out-of-date' system may not function quite as fast as the latest on the market but, provided a company adopted the right justification procedures, it will still perform the tasks for which it was purchased for many years. It is, of course, possible to update computers regularly, replacing certain key components of any system to keep the hardware at the forefront of technology. The justification for this approach must be made in the knowledge that it will cause some disruption and may provide only a minimal improvement in system performance as a whole.

A similar growth in the quality and variety of peripheral devices is also apparent and this often means that the device a company purchased a year ago is now available on the market at half the price. Again the justification should be that it was bought to give competitive advantage and therefore payback was considered in the light of its original price. However, most users will learn lessons about each device within weeks of installation. Each will have its own idiosyncrasies and methods will be adopted to accommodate these into the normal work of the organization. Consequently the value of any peripheral is not based solely on cost but also on practical experience.

Software is updated even more frequently than hardware and this in turn demands the attention of CAD/CAM users. Often new features based on user feedback are included in later releases of software and can offer companies significant savings in time as well as offering new approaches to problems. Sometimes the installation of a new software module can save hours and therefore justification for investing can be simple. Most suppliers offer maintenance and upgrade policies that include the installation of new software as it is produced. Managers should keep a watching brief on the functions available in other systems (both specialist and general purpose) to ensure that new features that may benefit the business can be added to existing packages.

There comes a time when any CAD/CAM system is old and needs replacing. The analogy is with cars: after a number of years spare parts become difficult to find and mechanical components break down. The fuel for a CAD/CAM system is not petrol but software and this is a commodity that is upgraded regularly. Developers have to try and rationalize the need for their product to run on older hardware with the desire to capitalize on newer capabilities. After a time they have to make the decision to stop work geared to the older systems and let them slowly decay. Maintenance charges inevitably increase as systems get older and there is not yet a market for vintage CAD/CAM packages! A continual upgrade policy is one way by which maintenance costs are contained. Another reason for upgrade is the need to overcome bottlenecks, often the very reason that a system was installed in the first place. It is evident in many companies that certain parts of the system work much faster than others and bottlenecks occur while waiting for printer or plotter output.

It is sensible for CAD/CAM users to visit shows and conferences, even after installation. These events help them to identify alternative approaches to design and they often benefit from the opportunity to discuss ideas with attendees from other organizations.

If a company makes the decision to replace the central computer at the heart of any CAD/CAM system the first observation will be an improvement in the system response time. The same observation applies to devices like printers and plotters: the newer the device the better the performance both in speed and in quality of output. Another example of an upgrade may be the use of colour screens for pattern design, lay planning and marker making: the early systems used only monochrome displays but the advent of inexpensive colour enabled them to show different sizes in different colours and therefore make work easier for the user.

One obvious reason for upgrade is the need to interconnect CAD/CAM with other systems. Sometimes companies have invested in more than one system (often from different manufacturers), for example one is for the design room and one used for production. Data is probably exchanged between them using floppy disks or magnetic tapes, and the usual upgrade path is the installation of a computer network so the two can exchange data electronically. Manual exchange of data between systems requires the software at one end to write data on to the transfer medium and at the other to read it into the target computer. Both these exercises can take time (a matter of minutes) and over a week this can easily amount to three or four working hours. The direct connection concept can be extended to other components of the CAD/CAM facility, notably any production machinery that accepts input on media other than by electronic connection.

The next interconnection option is to systems and processes that feed into CAD/CAM or extract data from the design or production processes. The options for this type of expansion are discussed in Chapter 7. Despite the relative ease of connection there are frequently problems with incompatibility between data: a textile design produced on one system cannot necessarily be read on another. Suppliers are slowly becoming less parochial about their data formats and it is now usually possible to send data from one system to another using an 'open data' policy.

With any upgrade or replacement strategy the option exists to change supplier and this is becoming a leading issue in the competitiveness of individual manufacturers. The concept of transferable data is now relatively straightforward and it is possible to choose to upgrade a facility by installing completely new hardware and software whilst transferring the existing data through an intermediate translation process. Obviously this has the disadvantage that staff need additional training but once they have mastered one system it does not take too long to understand and utilize the features of another.

THE COST OF NOT INVESTING

Perhaps the most important consideration is not the investment that has to be made in the purchase of CAD/CAM, but the potential for staying in business without the technology! Perhaps the biggest reason to invest in CAD/CAM is to remain competitive in the world market. Not having the technology may have certain short-term capital advantages but it may be a barrier to future business. It is the ability to merge quick response, high design content, flexibility and high quality with all the other elements that make a company attractive to its customers. Value for money (and not low cost) is being demanded by the retailers and those organizations able to offer this are the ones who will thrive into the twenty-first century.

Many of the most successful CAD/CAM users have developed new markets since the introduction of the technology. As their users become more competent with IT and as their own productivity increases so they are able to use more of their creative energies in the creation of new products. A few managers have realized the power in the IT systems and are using it as another means of gaining business. In general the ability to link electronically to customers via EDI systems has been proven to save paperwork and improve response times, but the real use of the concept has yet to begin. As well as using systems to transfer text-based ordering data the systems can be used to transfer designs in the form of CAD data and can also generate production information in CAM form for transmission to a remote site. There is an inherent cost saving in the use of electronic media to exchange data: media charges are reduced or eliminated, couriers or postal charges are non-existent and the time taken for delivery is measured in seconds, not hours or days. In a quick response culture there need be not only cost savings but also business benefits: being able to offer a speedy service means that companies can meet retail deadlines and therefore become preferred suppliers.

One bureau in London offers a grading and marker making service to its clients but generally does not plot out markers in its offices. Instead the information is generated locally and then sent electronically to site for plotting at the point of manufacture. Not only does this save the time and cost of transporting paper-based materials but it also allows the manufacturing company to schedule plots to coincide with manufacturing capacity. There is a vast saving in the omission of duplicated work: using electronic communication guarantees instant input to the grading and marker making process without the need to digitize patterns. This saves significant amounts of time and also avoids any errors in transcription thereby guaranteeing accuracy.

Companies are starting to see the possibilities for exploiting the technology in ways that complement their existing procedures: using portable systems as sales aids will minimize the paperwork that is necessary for each order and will allow staff to send orders from remote sites. Others want to add multimedia catalogues to the portfolio for each representative or to use the same concept on stands at shows and exhibitions. Without the technology these opportunities do not exist. The true cost of not investing will be measured by survival: only those businesses able to service the demands of the market will stay in business in the twenty-first century and this means that investment in computer technology is vital.

CASE STUDIES

Perhaps the best examples of CAD/CAM users are the leading UK suppliers to the high street retailers. Organizations like Courtaulds, Coats Viyella, Bairdwear, SR Gent and Dewhirsts all have systems for design and production. These companies have all invested significantly in the technology and all have learned lessons about its value and true cost.

Bairdwear is a good example of a company that has had to address problems regarding support and integration of systems from different suppliers. At one of its factories it has systems from Gerber and CDI for colour work that include all forms of textile simulation, packaging and labelling design as well as sample fabric production. It also has CAD/CAM systems for pattern making (from Assyst) and computer-controlled cutters from Gerber. The capital investment in these systems is significant and both hardware and software have to be upgraded regularly.

An observer of the Bairdwear systems will be highly impressed both with the amount of equipment and with the uses to which it is put. This is evidence of the investment the company has made in its staff and its culture. First, it has integrated the systems together: exchanging data between Gerber Artworks and CDI is not a trivial exercise and those organizations without a good understanding of file formats, computer-operating systems, communications and data storage systems will have trouble emulating the Bairdwear set-up. Second, it has trained its users to identify the package(s) most appropriate to each task: this means they use the best tools for each job, sometimes swapping between systems during development. The capacity to choose systems is a positive benefit to the designers, but only because the company has invested in the links that make it possible.

The work undertaken in the development of patterns is also impressive. Data developed on the Assyst configuration is passed in electronic form to a program (written in-house) that converts it to Gerber format to control the cutting machine. This program also displays the cutting information in graphical form on the machine itself, offering the operators a clear picture of the lay plan. It also means that each piece is appropriately labelled.

This particular factory cuts garments for other parts of the group and requests for work arrive in electronic form from external sites. Once in place this forms a natural part of the operation but there is a need for on-site expertise to support the activities.

To Bairdwear the true cost of CAD/CAM includes training, support and maintenance as well as software and hardware development and integration. It employs full-time staff for this activity but the benefits in terms of improved efficiency, responsiveness and dynamism far outweigh the additional costs.

Another company that has invested heavily in CAD/CAM is Coats Viyella. This group has Gerber systems for pattern making, and a design room that is highly computerized. In addition to a range of CDI systems used for textile design, packaging and labelling it has a Stork printer that is used to create samples of printed fabrics that are used to manufacture garments to present to clients. This process gives the company a significant advantage over its competitors when demonstrating new ideas to clients.

Like many other large organizations CV has specialist technical staff who assist in the configuration and maintenance of the hardware and software. One of the keys to the company's success is personnel related: the facility is managed by a computer literate designer who understands both the technology and the needs of the clients. She has a highly developed sense of creativity and channels her energies into the exploitation of the technology. Whole sample garments can be created within a day, incorporating both new textile prints and original pattern shapes. This facility could be replicated in many other organizations but the use of people and the investment in their knowledge is second to none.

Successful use of CAD is not limited to the large manufacturers: retailers use the technology for planning their product ranges and specifying their requirements. Debenhams, Evans, Principles, Top Shop and the other members of the old Burton Group all use the Prima CAD system in their head office for design work. Their investment in technology is not limited to the individual systems but extends to the provision of scanners and colour printers as well as to the computer networks that link users electronically. As with most other large organizations the users are supported by internal IT services provided by computer experts. During the integration phase of the CAD installation the organization recognized the need for product specialists, especially in response to the vast amount of data being generated by users, most of it in pictorial form. The resulting load on a traditional IT network could have been catastrophic had the team not had the foresight to ensure the right provision of storage and cabling for each user. For this organization the integration of CAD had major cost implications for the underlying IT infrastructure and in the knowledge required of its support staff.

A very different example of a CAD/CAM user is the Fashion Service for Disabled People based near Bradford. This organization specializes in the design and manufacture of clothing for individuals who find it difficult to purchase clothing 'off the peg'. A recent award of money from the Lotteries Charities Board has allowed the company to invest in a computer system to assist in its work and computerize the pattern construction process. A standard system coupled to a sample cutting machine is installed in its facility and this is linked to different centres around the country where specialist clothing advisers are located. Each specialist meets clients and takes the appropriate measurements, which are entered into a computer terminal linked to the Bradford centre. The CAD/CAM facility processes these measurements using specialist software written for the centre and outputs the data to the CAD facility for style development and automatic cutting. In addition to the capital cost of the equipment the centre has invested in a technical manager whose role is to maintain the facility and to develop specialist software to complement the standard facilities so that 'made-to-measure' facilities can be offered to clients around the country.

6

HUMAN ISSUES

❖

It does not matter how clever, efficient or easy to use a CAD/CAM system is, the ultimate determining factor is human. Success or failure usually depends on people, not equipment. Moreover, it is not just the operators of CAD who are responsible for its exploitation: their managers and colleagues must all play their part. To capitalize fully on the technology, cultural and managerial issues need to be included in the training and integration processes.

Some companies use their systems as an integrated part of their manufacturing process: patterns are stored on the system, modified to produce new styles, graded across the required size range, linked together in the required ratios to make markers and then cut using computer-controlled machinery. Others use them for specific tasks only such as bra grading and fabric estimation. Clothing manufacturers with systems for design often use them purely for illustration and the creation of marketing and packaging ideas. Textile manufacturers will frequently have direct links from pictorial information to their production machinery, be it for knitting, weaving or printing processes.

In all these cases success relies not so much on which system they have installed, more on the ways in which it is used. The information stored in a system can be processed in a variety of ways, and these depend on the company and the operators. CAD/CAM systems are only as good as their users, and the examples of good practice come from those who are well organized and can see how systems and processes can be linked together.

Personnel within the industry generally lack the mix of talents, education and experience necessary to design their own software and configure their own systems. As computer users they often accept limitations within the hardware and software that could be overcome with a greater level of understanding. This is slowly changing as the more experienced CAD/CAM operators push the technology beyond its prescribed limits.

There are many people who doubt the technology. Some are cautious because they have invested in the past and have not reaped the big rewards that they had anticipated; others are wary due to lack of knowledge or fear of redundancy. What is clear, however, is that the introduction of CAD does not de-skill operations nor is it a replacement for talent. What it does most obviously is to free designers from time-consuming, repetitive tasks and allows them more time to experiment, to improve quality and to research their market. A CAD system will enable designers to spend more time being creative, either producing more output or increasing the quality of their work.

Good pattern cutters are still in great demand but there is an increasing tendency for colleges to produce 'fashion' graduates who do not fully understand the relationships between patterns and the human body. The engineering skills that link geometry to the human form are a scarce commodity. A pattern manipulation CAD system used by someone who does not have this understanding will produce no better results than are possible with manual methods. The same applies to the grading process: although the systems can produce the nests of individual pattern pieces in a few seconds the fit of each size depends on how well the grading rules accommodate the change in size and shape of the human form across the spectrum of individuals that they are trying to fit.

CAD/CAM forms part of the ever-increasing use of information technology in clothing and textiles companies and its influence is spreading. The computer technologies are creating new career opportunities and, in addition to CAD/CAM operators, multimedia programmers, producers and designers are in demand. An increasing number of companies are realizing the value of the electronic medium and are starting to exploit its capability. Teams of creative people with a mix of talents are being employed to produce catalogues and to design themes, presentations and sales material. Some have a computer background, others come from clothing and textiles disciplines while others come from a graphic design environment. Such multidisciplinary teams are going to become increasingly common.

TRAINING AND SUPPORT

Training is essential to the successful exploitation of any CAD/CAM system. In fact training should not be thought of as an exercise that is undertaken at or around the time of installation: it should be considered as an exercise that occurs throughout a user's career.

Training is often envisaged as an introduction to a system. As such it begins well before installation of the system. During the sales phase when companies are producing their shortlist of vendors they should have gained a general understanding of the principles that characterize the systems. As they refine their choice of companies it is hoped that 'real' tasks are performed as the measure of confidence and capability in the selected supplier. It is important to involve potential users of the system in these final stages, which in fact form the initial training needs. Users of a system should have a practical 'feel' for its capabilities and for the devices it employs before installation.

There are many aspects to training and, of course, the initial element is usually timed to coincide with installation. The cost of this training is normally built into the system quotation. Sometimes it is for work to be undertaken at the supplier's offices, otherwise it is undertaken on-site. The choice of location can affect the cost (travel, accommodation, etc.) and can therefore limit the number of participants. It is essential that companies train adequate staff to allow for sickness, retirement and resignation so that there is always a suitable operator available and therefore someone who can train others.

Another consideration, especially in larger companies, is the selection of staff for training: some may have more natural aptitude for the technology than others and therefore may be considered as the natural candidates for the first training sessions. In turn they can train others internally as and when time permits. There are many examples of companies where the aptitude of internal staff was such that there was no need to recruit personnel specially to run CAD/CAM facilities. Indeed, most of the examples of best practice come from organizations where CAD/CAM capability has been developed from within. Managers should be warned about the difference between slickness and real understanding: although a user may appear to be highly proficient on the operation of a system's basic functions they may not use its filing and library functions well and may therefore not be capitalizing on the full benefits a system can offer.

The same warning applies to the use of jargon. Many so-called 'experts' have little in-depth knowledge of the technology but use terminology to enhance their reputation. Real experts will be able to translate technical terms into ones that their managers can grasp without the need for a detailed understanding of the system's lowest-level functions. Managers themselves should get involved in some of the training sessions, simply to appreciate the mechanics of the operation and therefore use the experience to assess the resources (time and manpower) that each task should demand.

A number of sensible tactics can be adopted when determining training needs. The first is to identify which members of staff are to be involved in the process. All users should be given appropriate time to learn the basic skills and therefore with a single system it is sensible to organize training in groups of no more than three. Often one-to-one sessions are even more effective, especially as training can be directed towards each individual's own role. One simple point to remember is that users need sufficient time to practise their skills between training sessions: if all contact with the trainer is concentrated in lectures and simple exercises much of it will be wasted.

Sometimes group sessions can be used to identify particular problems or to identify methods of working that best reflect the company's own practice.

Part of the requirement of a training course is to familiarize users with the function of the hardware as well as the software and so topics like loading and unloading paper from printers and plotters will be covered. So, too, will the settings of any input equipment (scanners and cameras in particular). The mechanical set-up of each device can take a disproportionate amount of time and users should ensure that they gain competence during the training sessions. They will be trained on what action to take when something malfunctions and how to liaise with the support team.

A training plan needs to incorporate far more than the mechanical use of each product. All staff need to understand how their particular use of the system(s) contributes to the general efficiency of the company and this demands training in attitudes as well as operation. Users must learn enough about the system's filing system to avoid duplication or errors such as deleting another person's data or accidentally updating a master file (this can occur even with security protection).

All suppliers offer system support and this should be used whenever necessary. As internal staff become more competent users of the system their local knowledge is likely to be able to resolve the majority of user problems and solve them more quickly than the supplier as they are familiar with the installation and its normal operation. It is therefore sensible for any organization with an IT strategy to form a user group and to nominate individuals as primary points of contact for internal staff as well as external suppliers and consultants. If interested employees are encouraged to gain computer systems and networks knowledge by a combination of 'hands on' experience and formal training courses the more a company will be able to manage its own IT infrastructure. Training and development of internal staff is an important consideration for businesses looking for Investors in People (IIP) accreditation.

Users need appropriate support from within the organization as well as from the supplier throughout their initiation phase. Some of the worst examples of system use come from companies where managers expect designers to become instant experts and produce output overnight. Investment in user training and support is essential and the biggest benefits are generally gained when the installation of a system is planned properly and users are involved throughout the selection and installation processes.

WORKPLACE LAYOUT AND ORGANIZATION

Some factory and workplace layouts defy logical description! Many have grown in an unstructured manner and often new managers have inherited their predecessor's problems. The introduction of a CAD/CAM system will often follow the execution of an IT audit (based on the subjects covered in Chapter 3) and one element of the report should be the clarification of the logistical flow of information and product around the factory. Sometimes the very nature of an existing set-up introduces inefficiencies and contributes to reduced staff morale. Systems that defy logic are difficult to justify and often only fiscal restrictions are put forward as the reasons for retaining them. Introducing CAD/CAM is not cheap but although it cannot solve fundamental problems, it can be used as a catalyst for change throughout the organization.

Businesses with more than one site are particularly vulnerable to organizational problems: some parts may be seen as the successful contributors while others may feel isolated. The use of an integrated IT strategy with suitable connections between all sites should have the effect of bringing staff together in a broad, 'virtual' organization that shares its data between sites. Managers will be able to measure performance directly and will be able to identify their own strengths and weaknesses when compared to their partners.

Where multi-sited businesses have been created by take-overs and mergers there will inevitably be different working practices at each location and the adoption of an integrated IT strategy can be one way in which these are amalgamated and the resulting methods monitored to ensure they are efficiently used. Each site is likely to have particular strengths and weaknesses – some may be well positioned to recruit school leavers and may have NVQ training facilities, others may have particular pieces of equipment that allow them to offer special facilities to their customers. It is important for all such companies to trade on their strengths and to share information between locations to capitalize on their good points.

Although good team spirit is an essential company strength it is also an inherent weakness as information that is traded during discussions relies heavily on internal knowledge and well-proven work practice. The installation of CAD/CAM is often an excellent opportunity to review organization and structure. Existing IT systems are often not capable of assisting management in decision-making debates and the integration of CAD/CAM with other systems and processes can create significant efficiency improvements.

An example may demonstrate the far-reaching nature of the use of information: a comprehensive list of assembly instructions is supplied to each operative, showing how each manufacturing step is to be performed. This list is usually supplied in manual form and is presented as a combination of diagrams, photographs and written text. It includes details of any safety precautions that need to be adopted when the operations are executed. It is produced as an integral part of the company's own training procedures and is an obvious contributor to inherently high quality standards. The information content needs continual update and is a barrier when new styles are introduced. As distribution relies on each operative filing the new instructions it is likely that mistakes will be made and not all instruction books will be identical. Although this is a human error it could easily be resolved by using electronic manuals, each updated from a central source, using screens at each station to display the instructions.

Companies try to minimize their work in progress and keep the smallest possible amount of finished goods as these items all represent capital that is tied up, yet all companies have to consider the needs of their customers, especially the large retailers who demand regular call-off deliveries from bulk orders. Again the use of a well-organized IT system can facilitate planning across all sites, allowing one to assist another at peak times, minimizing stock levels whilst maintaining delivery schedules.

The more a company uses electronic communication the more it will rely on IT systems, and local knowledge is invaluable when faults occur. As the company becomes more streamlined and able to monitor all aspects of selling, design, production and delivery it will find that many of the monitoring points needed for ISO 9000 (or BS 5750) registration are in place.

TEAMWORKING

To complement technology change a number of companies are also making strides towards cultural change. It is becoming ever more evident that companies need to plan for change and that they have to offer a dynamic approach to the demands of the market. Today's market requires managers who themselves are flexible, dynamic and well versed in all aspects of production, retail and technology. This requires improved and continuing education and training throughout their professional career. CAD/CAM training must apply to all levels of user and manager in a company.

One of the main business drivers in any company is efficiency and projects centred on two or three universities are assisting companies to improve their competitiveness, reduce their costs and enhance their quality by means of changes in working practice and management structure. A simple example is the introduction of 'teamworking', whereby work in progress is minimized and the experience and intelligence of each team is used to speed the production of new designs through the factory. To those unfamiliar with this concept the main feature is the removal of long assembly lines with operators performing individual functions (e.g. one puts sleeves into a jacket body and the next inserts the collar), replacing them with many small teams (typically 5 or 6 people), each group producing complete garments.

The advantages of this scheme are extensive and include the following points:

O   Quality standards are improved
O   New garments can be introduced into the production schedule very quickly.
O   Teams are naturally self-supporting and self-motivating

○   Absenteeism is reduced
○   Work in progress is reduced significantly
○   The experience of the operators is used to overcome manufacturing
        problems

At a seminar in Greece in 1993 one company (Marathon Knitwear) sent five of its staff (four teamworking operatives and their supervisor) to demonstrate the methods and practical organization of a 'quick response' team. They were given a set of sewing machines, the pattern pieces (ready cut out), the appropriate threads and buttons and within half an hour of arrival they had produced the first garment. They found problems with poorly cut patterns and were able to point out the mistakes before the next batch was supplied, thereby improving quality standards and correcting problems at their source rather than making do. They trimmed excess material at the point of assembly, ensuring that seams fitted correctly and garments hung correctly.

With a highly flexible, competent workforce companies will frequently find that their overall structure and organization can be reviewed. The ability to manufacture a variety of goods fast and to a high standard demands that managers are capable of feeding the teams with complete agreement assemblies. As soon as a company can offer quick response production there will be pressures to offer quick response design too. It is easy to demonstrate exactly how quickly fashion designers using CAD/CAM systems can produce patterns ready for manufacture. With computerized pattern modification, grading and marker making this process can be reduced to just an hour or two.

CONTINUING EDUCATION

There is still only minimal use of CAD/CAM systems for clothing and textiles design and production in colleges and universities. There are a number of reasons for this, top of the list being the amount of investment needed to equip a studio with adequate facilities for a complete class to use. This is slowly changing as systems become more common and as suppliers are willing to sell site licences at low cost to educational establishments. Staff in colleges need to be trained on systems and there is a growing recognition of the need for regular updating and development courses, sometimes involving industrial secondment. This is very exciting and stimulating for academic staff as it allows them both to increase their own skills and knowledge and to identify the key issues that should be included in the syllabus that they teach to their students.

There are a few new initiatives based around colleges and universities devoted to the training and education of personnel in the industry, centred on the recognition of GNVQ qualifications. These projects are assembling suitable equipment and staff in centres devoted to training and education. In addition to the provision of 'hands on' CAD/CAM courses they offer access to some of the latest technologies including multimedia and video conferencing.

There is, of course, a need for continuing update, education and training for in-company staff and there are plentiful opportunities for individuals to brief themselves by attending shows, conferences and exhibitions. Events like ITMA, IMB and Clotech are seen as the showcases for the big players and they are generally used as the launchpad for new products. Other conferences like the Textile Institute's 'Investing in Design by Computer' series offer serious advice based on practical experience in many companies. These events are equally valuable to practitioners and managers – to the former it may be learning new techniques and analytical approaches that is most beneficial, to the latter it may be the ability to capitalize on new market creation or improved efficiency.

Bodies like the Department of Trade and Industry and the British Clothing Industry Association are continuing to evaluate the generic needs of the industry and are developing policies to support the education of individuals who are able to exploit the technology and contribute to national and international competitiveness. Overriding their considerations is a need to ensure that as many people as possible are aware of the technology, its capabilities and cost so that investment decisions can be made on sensible grounds.

So much of the success of any company depends on its personnel that it makes sense to consider how individuals approach the technology and what level of understanding they require or attain. Some find they like the medium in its own right and they capitalize on its capability, treating the technology as a new set of tools to be used in addition to their existing ones. These individuals are the creative drivers of the technology and their results often surprise and delight the suppliers, showing how a system can be used in creative ways that defy normal practice and exploit lateral thinking. Others find the discipline of filing and retrieving alien and resist the technology. In every case there is a need for continual education, especially in the area of computer storage, data representation and hardware control. It is important to realize that individuals need training in the management of information as well as in the use of information technology.

NEW SKILLS

Staff are the key component in the success of any CAD/CAM system. Nowadays businesses are expected to invest in staff development and individuals are encouraged to maintain their own career development records. One item that will need to appear on a curriculum vitae is a knowledge of CAD/CAM systems and therefore companies without the technology are likely to lose staff to their competitors. There is a contradiction in this argument though: one of the first organizations to invest in CAD views the staff situation from a different perspective. Its studio manager was quoted in 1993 as saying that she had trained about 50 per cent of the CAD users in the country, many of them now working for her competitors. Being a trailblazer does not always lead to staff loyalty once opportunities are seen elsewhere.

CAD/CAM competence opens new avenues for career development provided managers are sufficiently far-sighted to realize the opportunities that the technology offers. In addition to performing routine design and production tasks the technology can be used in other areas such as sales promotion and training. The users of CAD/CAM systems will be even more technically literate and design aware: we are about to see the emergence of a new type of individual in the clothing world – the clothing computer expert. These individuals will be experts in the design and manufacture of garments as well as knowledgeable about the computer technology.

MANAGEMENT AND SKILLS ISSUES

Many companies employ a highly skilled and flexible workforce. Personnel are able to achieve results despite (rather than because of) existing IT systems. Orders cannot be chased once goods have been dispatched from the manufacturing plant and planning seems to be an unstructured activity based on little factual information and relying instead on experience and word-of-mouth communications. So much management has to be performed without access to up-to-the-minute information that a reactive approach is often adopted.

Empowerment is one means to improve a company's performance. This strategy demands that accurate, current data is provided to many personnel, enabling everyone to plan better and to be more responsive to customers. The act of empowerment means a delegation of authority and responsibility and this, coupled with access to data, means the adoption of an 'open' data system with security rights as to who can read data, who can write it and who is barred from access. As well as needing personnel who can manage a computer network from a hardware and software point of view there also needs to be a recognition of the role of a manager who establishes security and insurance mechanisms. Companies wanting to exploit IT will need to appoint personnel with the relevant skills.

There is an opportunity for personnel issues to form part of an IT strategy: in addition to the obvious need to provide payroll functions the proper integration of personnel records will allow an analysis of the elements concerning human factors of the business to be performed. This data can include records of expertise and training for all staff as well as recording absence and discipline matters.

In some cases the adoption of an integrated IT strategy will require significant changes in management structure and responsibility. Having access to up-to-the minute data about company performance will place more responsibility on good decision makers. This may change traditional power balances and job responsibilities. Ownership of systems and processes will have to be made clear and will depend on access to central data. Excuses cannot be based on the 'I didn't receive the paperwork in time' response. Staff will have to learn to share tasks and trust one another. Adopting cultural change is an essential element of an integrated IT strategy.

ESTABLISHING AN IT DEPARTMENT

With so much emphasis placed on IT systems the question of creating an IT department becomes worthy of consideration. Undoubtedly the biggest need within a company is for staff understanding of the IT system software, data, hardware and communications links. This requires training, clear management and high quality, well-motivated personnel.

The exact nature of any IT specialist's role depends on the size and structure of a company but it should be recognized that centralized teams in larger organizations are rarely able to respond effectively to the needs of their users. This is particularly true when CAD/CAM systems are introduced: many computer experts are unfamiliar with specialist systems. Decentralization, locating support staff with the users, is becoming a proven policy.

To create the right team for IT systems to provide full benefits to all personnel there needs to be a clear delineation of responsibility and any specialist staff need to be integrated into the rest of the workforce. The 'experts' on any elements of the main computer and network infrastructure should be readily accessible and must be approachable. To this end it is sensible for them to be located near to the main areas of activity (e.g. the sales office or the design room) so that they continue to appreciate the work of the company and the role of the computer system(s) as an enabling technology. They need to operate a fault finding/fixing service and must therefore become familiar with the main facilities and the specialist equipment.

The most authoritative person on any CAD/CAM system is normally the main user and he or she soon becomes expert at diagnosing faults. This type of individual sometimes needs support from internal personnel on more fundamental issues like disk crashes or incompatible data formats. If the users and the technology specialists form good working relationships the formality of an IT department may be unnecessary but their role must not be overlooked. Sometimes the need for in-house staff becomes apparent only when support from external bodies becomes unresponsive or when internal faults occur more frequently than expected. More often there is a realization that other companies are using their IT systems in a more effective manner and a desire to become more pro-active users surfaces.

Assuming a company can justify the need for an IT specialist then five main topics should be considered in the appointment of staff: system software, user programs, data, hardware, and communications and networks. Of extreme importance is the need for visionary management and motivation: the IT staff must share goals with the board and must both complement their activity and provide additional opportunity.

Checklist

○   Can the company justify the appointment of an IT specialist?
○   Consider the best location for any IT support personnel
○   Make sure managers are kept aware of IT opportunities

SYSTEM SOFTWARE

Staff need a sound knowledge of the central computer operating system(s) such as MS-DOS, UNIX or Windows. This will enable them to assess a large number of technical issues, especially when it comes to sharing information or establishing users. They will need to understand low-level system functions (e.g. why a serial port is not working) as well as higher-level organization (e.g. file structure and system security). If a network is installed then a good working knowledge of it must also be included on the staff credentials.

Checklist

○   Ensure that staff have a good knowledge of all the system software
○   Ensure that staff understand high-level and low-level functions of the system operation
○   Ensure that staff have a good understanding of file structures, standards and security
○   Ensure that staff are able to support links to external computer systems

USER PROGRAMS

There are two types of user software – the first covers 'off-the-shelf' packages like Microsoft Excel, Adobe Photoshop, Gerber's Accumark and Corel Draw that can be accessed by users as tools to assist their own development work; the second includes applications written for specific functions (like a database) which may be produced internally or be commissioned from external sources.

In the case of the first group the user manuals (and installation instructions they contain) should provide enough data to allow IT staff to configure systems correctly. Unfortunately some packages are not compatible with others and this requires the installer to have system configuration knowledge to resolve difficulties such as memory conflicts, different screen resolutions or a variety of modem set-ups. The combinations are too many to include but, especially in the PC world, this type of problem is commonplace (despite the so-called standards like Windows 95).

Often specially written software will have developed over its lifetime and in many companies the product documentation is inadequate. This frequently precludes easy upgrade of either hardware or software. Companies need to acknowledge the need for ownership of their own software and should recruit staff who are good at software documentation as well as programming. This will often place a burden on those who have to supervise staff with technical knowledge outside the manager's normal field.

Since the quality and performance of so many software tools improves every year, internal software needs to develop rapidly too, capitalizing on new and improved features in the underlying tools. This prevents internal software from becoming unresponsive, inflexible and staid. It also means that IT staff have to maintain regular contact with the market and will need to read books and magazines as well as attending trade fairs and exhibitions.

At all times staff must be instructed to ensure data structures are clearly defined and that interoperability is a prerequisite to all software purchase and development.

Checklist

O   Ensure that staff understand how to install, configure and use all 'off-the-shelf' packages

O   Ensure that staff have comprehensive knowledge of all operating systems

O   Set documentation standards for all internal development work

O   Allow staff to keep abreast of developments in software and hardware by encouraging them to visit shows and read technical journals

O   Ensure interconnectivity between systems and processes by making sure staff are aware of standards and good working practices

O   Provide managers with sufficient training for them to supervise IT staff

DATA

From a management point of view it is essential that IT systems are flexible enough to provide information in a form suitable for individual requirements. Good managers take an 'ownership' of data with the knowledge that it can be interrogated and presented in a variety of ways. They demand that their IT systems are flexible enough to respond in the most efficient manner for each request. This attitude towards data is to be commended as it recognizes the difference between 'information' and 'data' and generally highlights the use of technology to interrogate the latter to provide the former.

IT staff need to ensure that they can build databases that are open and flexible with the ability to generate summaries according to a wide variety of requirements. Graphical options are frequently used as an effective and state-of-the-art presentation method.

Checklist

O   Ensure that staff are able to provide reports in appropriate formats and in clearly defined procedural ways

O   Ensure that managers are able to specify fully the type of enquiries they wish to make of their IT systems so that reporting and formatting issues can be correctly established

O   Ensure that data structures adhere to standards wherever possible

HARDWARE

The majority of IT systems use standard components (e.g. laser printers and modems) that can be bought inexpensively from a wide range of suppliers. Therefore it is not always sensible to have a hardware support policy that costs more than the off-the-shelf replacement of a set of components. There is little point in recruiting staff to perform hardware maintenance and repair: either the equipment they require is too specialized (and therefore expensive) or the time it would take to fix means that it is cheaper to junk the faulty element and purchase new. Consequently companies should use the support and maintenance services offered by their hardware suppliers. IT staff do, however, need to know a lot about fault diagnosis, about hardware configuration and about performance optimization. They should act as the front-line support within any company and should be able to rectify the majority of problems on the spot.

Certain new technologies such as video conferencing and multimedia will become part of IT systems over the next few years and it will be necessary to ensure that personnel are able to adapt their hardware and systems knowledge to encompass such equipment.

Checklist

O   Ensure that staff are trained on all aspects of fault diagnosis

O   Ensure that staff are able to configure hardware to give optimal performance

COMMUNICATIONS AND NETWORKS

The big requirement of the late twentieth century in any IT-based organization is for quality telecommunications to link systems and processes. This requires high calibre staff who understand not only all the hardware and software of the computer systems themselves but also the means (again covering hardware and software) by which they are interconnected. On a single site this means that staff need good knowledge of network architecture and messaging protocols (local area networks), across more than one location this requirement is extended to wide area network experience.

The local area network, on one site, will provide all users with access to data: the initial challenge is to use one device (probably a PC) to act both as a computer for each user's processing needs and as a terminal that can access centralized systems. There are many difficult tasks in trying to remove the old concept of 'dumb terminals' that simply provide data (in the form of text) to the user. Modern systems expect the format of data to reflect individual needs, using graphics where appropriate.

Possibly the biggest challenge to any business is the establishment of multi-site communications with links that offer access to information both inside and outside the organization. Within one distributed company this will mean that remote sites will be able to check warehouse stock, to access library information and to establish costing data. For suppliers and customers it opens the possibility for a truly interactive design and production discussion based on shared data and common goals.

To achieve any level of success staff will need to become familiar with communications equipment (modems, bridges, routers, switches, etc.) as well as the more familiar computing components. There is a shortage of graduates with practical telecommunications and computer experience and therefore it is unlikely that staff already in post will have detailed knowledge. Every opportunity to send staff on training courses outside the organization should be used to enable the company to streamline its network and to provide the optimal functions to each user.

A bewildering array of telecommunications equipment and service is available to the consumer. Terms like 'modems', 'ISDN' and 'ATM' all mean a lot to the experts but to most IT users they are just jargon. It is imperative that businesses identify the information they wish to share and then specify the response time they require (is it micro seconds, minutes or hours) so that the appropriate grade of link can be established.

Checklist

O   Use every opportunity to train staff on computer networks and telecommunications links

O   Identify the ways in which information can be shared with internal staff

O   Investigate market opportunities that can be exploited by the provision of external links to suppliers and customers, noting particularly the response times that are required

7

INTEGRATING CAD/CAM WITH OTHER IT SYSTEMS

❖

Different companies have adopted different approaches to IT yet all have evidence of similar problems. These difficulties relate primarily to the lack of a visionary strategy for the use of information as a commodity that is passed between systems and processes. With the exception of a minimal amount of computer technology used for CAD/CAM work the majority of IT investment has been made in systems for sales order processing, stock control and payroll production. There is little evidence of IT use in forward planning, nor of systems being used for the analysis of design performance. Even the use of EDI (electronic data interchange) is only just beginning.

There are, of course, many other uses of information technology in the industry, some of which are used to provide input to CAD/CAM. More and more companies are starting to exploit these links as a means of becoming ever more responsive to market demands. The use of electronic point of sale (EPOS) terminals has revolutionized the understanding of retail patterns and has effectively removed the warehouse. Stores now operate on the principle of ordering to meet demand, which has changed the relationship between retailers and manufacturers.

The term 'logistics' has generally been interpreted as the means by which goods are delivered but it should be interpreted in a broader context to include the whole process of ensuring the right goods are in the right place at the right time. The retailers themselves use data gathered from EPOS systems in a multiplicity of ways, one of which is to assist planning and ordering. To ensure that the manufacturers are able to respond quickly to trends in the high street this retail data must be shared with the supply chain.

In the manufacturing companies there are also many other IT systems, notably those used for stock control. Databases maintain records of fabrics, accessories and so on so that manufacturing can rely on the availability of all

95

components to meet the retailer's demands. These databases can be linked to ordering systems so that lead times for stock are built in to any planning exercises. Clearly garment manufacturers need to predict market trends and to use this data to ensure that they can cater for its demands. Fabric producers need similar guidelines and therefore the streamlining of the supply chain places significant emphasis on the sharing of retail and fashion trends in a form where they can be used appropriately: computer systems are the most obvious means to achieve this.

A plethora of systems like GSD (General Sewing Data – a system for estimating the labour element of garment assembly) are used to assist in the costing and estimating process. Often these link directly to CAD/CAM. They are generally used to identify the labour content of any garment production and are used extensively in larger companies. Other management products for assisting the planning process are available and slowly gaining credibility. These include software packages for establishing critical path analysis, production flows and payment systems.

LINKING CAD/CAM TO OTHER SYSTEMS

Many CAD/CAM users are great advocates for the technology but fail to capitalize on the complete potential of their systems, primarily because systems have not been integrated with other elements of the business.

The purchase of CAD/CAM systems can be justified on a number of self-contained grounds but it is becoming increasingly evident in companies that have already installed the technology that there are significant gains to be made by using CAD/CAM as part of a comprehensive information technology environment. The use of computers and telecommunications systems to pass information between systems and processes is an essential contributor to business success and the clothing and textiles industry can benefit from lessons learned in other market sectors.

The basic elements of any IT system are independent of any one package. Manufacturing data needs to be available around the shop floor, warehousing stock needs to be monitored and controlled, supplies need to be co-ordinated, and financial information must be available at all times. The significant features of an integrated system are a comprehensive understanding of the data formats required at each stage and a method by which information can be transferred. The former is often a simple matter of ensuring that standards are adopted and the latter may demand the installation of a network that links computers together.

The obvious area where CAD/CAM data can be used is in the production process: a company that employs manual cutting methods will take markers in the form of paper templates and use these as the source of its data. One using automatic methods will transfer the paper template (used to mark the name, size and orientation of each piece) and use a disk, tape or network to pass instructions in electronic form to the cutting machinery. There are many other areas where CAD/CAM data can be used to great effect: the minute a marker is created the exact fabric requirements are known and they can be used to check stock levels. An electronic link to a database can perform this task without human intervention. Designers themselves can check costings on their CAD terminals using the same links. Labels, production planning schedules, work tickets, etc. can all be produced from the data on a CAD/CAM system.

Input to a system is often in the form of existing paper-based material: textile design systems often use scanners as their primary input medium and pattern design systems use digitizing tablets to trace round shapes. However, once material has been input it is available for regular future reference and this means that designs can be used, modified and adapted simply by duplicating the original. Size charts (which in turn are used to produce grading rules) are generally supplied from retailers in paper form and have to be transcribed into computer systems. With CAD they can be received electronically, minimizing the time taken to input the data and avoiding accidental errors in the process. The same is true for dye recipes and the increasing use of Pantone standards for colour referencing means that the accurate communication of colour data around the world is becoming easier.

The process of identifying data exchange mechanisms is non-trivial and the implementation of any one task is often difficult, yet the principle is easy. CAD/CAM systems have been developed without internationally agreed standards yet many of them use standard computer hardware and software as their central element. Products like Microsoft Windows offer users the ability to exchange data very simply and images can now be imported and exported by many different packages. The same is not yet true of pattern data, nor of grading or marker making information. Although it is possible, an in-house expert is likely to be needed to capitalize on the potential for a fully integrated IT system.

Checklist

○   Identify all systems and processes internally where CAD/CAM data can be used
○   Identify all systems and processes that can supply data to CAD/CAM
○   Establish what links are possible with suppliers and customers
○   Set standards for data transfer

USING CAD/CAM SYSTEMS IN AN INTEGRATED ENVIRONMENT

No two CAD/CAM systems are used in identical fashion – although performing similar functions the methods by which results are achieved differ significantly between brands. Users of identical systems in different companies are likely to observe different working practices and therefore there are no simple rules for any company wishing to adopt the technology. The great advantage of any system is its ability to offer material in electronic as well as paper or other forms. Textile designers can sell their goods on disk or even via a telephone line so that the purchaser can immediately further process the idea. Linking systems and processes by providing computer-based data in the appropriate form is the means by which efficiency is improved, timescales reduced and competitiveness enhanced.

It took a long time for retailers to accept computer-generated artwork; the resistance was not broken down until the quality of colour printers took a quantum leap forward in the early 1990s. There is still a reluctance to accept electronic material, much of the resistance based on issues of copyright and originality. These are highly complex matters and not easily resolved but the attraction of the time-saving nature of an electronic purchase will soon generate working solutions. The fact that *Drapers Record* and Design Intelligence have produced products using CAD/CAM systems in CD form will provide the recognition of the value and potential of the medium.

Inevitably the influence of the larger retailers dominates the market and they are already making big strides towards electronic trading. Electronic data interchange (EDI) is commonly thought to mean paperless ordering and call-off transactions but it embodies a multiplicity of trading needs. Marks and Spencer has instigated a Contract Management System which takes the EDI concept into the realms of an information dissemination package. The aim is to improve the effectiveness of communication with its suppliers whilst minimizing the human interaction with paper-based systems. By specifying the type of equipment and functionality required at a supplier's premises it is possible to exploit the medium as a means by which specifications can be given, sales data exchanged, manufacturing standards set and design data transferred. Manufacturers will be forced into the introduction of this type of technology simply to remain on the approved supplier list. Initially this may seem an imposition but it is sure to save vast quantities of paperwork and improve the quality of data provision, and cost savings should be a direct result. The adoption of more integrated data exchange raises questions about security and integrity as well as intellectual property rights. All of these issues are under review by manufacturers and retailers in other industries and new laws and standards will emerge.

Other companies are using the Internet to promote their work and this is likely to be a growing trend. Those who have used the system will note how slow the response can be, especially when graphical data is used by the promoter. This is due to the infrastructure of the computer networks that are interconnected and this is being improved at great speed. Internet type promotion is the key development of the 1990s and represents a mixture of computer technology and telecommunications. As such the medium now exists for designers to capitalize on their creative talents and make the message visually stimulating.

One exciting concept behind the Internet is access to libraries around the world: users can visit collections of art from the comfort of their own desk, browsing the contents and purchasing copies of material as required. The same concept can be used internally and libraries of all internal material (pattern blocks, cutting plans, fabric stock, etc.) can be made available to all CAD/CAM users. The assumption is, of course, that all material is well categorized and users are aware of its existence. This demands a new philosophy of management, proclaiming 'open' access to data and recruiting people with good librarian skills to exploit material. Such organization would be of great benefit to the larger multi-site companies where functions and data are often duplicated to provide local access at each location. The concept of private, corporate and public information will have to be adopted and suitable access rights allocated by a system manager. The use of interconnected sites allows companies to set up electronic mail (e-mail), a means by which documents and their attachments may be exchanged.

One big problem with electronic connection is that it can stimulate only audio and video senses and any tactile quality is omitted. There are a number of ways round this limitation, one of which is the use of video conferencing systems in addition to e-mail. Users are able to see each other during their discourse and the camera can show material in action, allowing behavioural characteristics to be discussed and demonstrated between participants. Again, the great advantages of this type of interaction are speed and efficiency, especially when the users may be thousands of miles apart. Another solution is to use CAD/CAM systems to print directly on to cloth or to weave or knit samples at the required location from data generated remotely. For many companies the cost of this method is prohibitive but its use is spreading. It is of great value when a company can design both garment and fabric, produce samples and demonstrate its ideas in less than a day. The most obvious benefit is when opportunistic sales arise, reflecting a retailer's lack of merchandise in certain categories. It does, however, give another benefit and that is the ability to produce 'one-offs', either for customers or for promotional work.

Computer technology is no longer restricted to scientific applications and engineering environments. Since the mid-1980s there has been a revolution in the use of digital techniques across the graphic arts. Most printing is performed from desktop systems and photography is rapidly becoming less dependent on celluloid film with digital cameras becoming more popular. The newer concepts of multimedia and virtual reality are emerging as highly attractive technologies with wide ranges of application across many disciplines. Coupling computer-based technology with modern telecommunications systems makes teleworking and collaborative design possible and these ideas are set to revolutionize the traditional concepts of work practice.

As designers in the clothing and textiles industry adapt their methods to capitalize on the power of the latest systems they will soon be able to spend more time exercising their creative talents and less performing repetitive tasks. The increasing availability of information in digital form via CD-ROM publications and through the Internet means that computers can be used to source material and supply data in the form of text, pictures and video.

CAD/CAM systems form a natural part of the multimedia world: as data becomes a commodity traded between systems, CAD output can be incorporated into many multimedia products. 3D CAD is used as the basis for creating objects in virtual reality systems and computer simulation can be used to model all the factory floor processes.

Checklist

O   Identify the ways that designers gather, process and disseminate information
O   Consider improvements in the means by which designs are transferred to production and ensure that responsibilities are clearly defined
O   Which ancillary processes can benefit from integration with the mainstream activities of the design room?

INTEGRATING INFORMATION

The basic commodity in any CAD/CAM system is *information:* be it a set of geometric coordinates that describe a pattern shape, a series of coloured points that make up an illustration or a list of instructions that instruct a knitting machine how to form its stitches or change yarns, the rudimentary component is data. All any CAD/CAM system allows the user to do is process information – pattern shapes can be altered, illustrations re-coloured, stretched and squashed, and knitting machines programmed to produce different stitch formations. The great advantage of any system is that it performs these manipulations incredibly quickly, giving users time to experiment with their designs.

In the future the boundary between CAD/CAM systems and other processes (stock control, invoicing, EDI, etc.) will be less rigid. The primary reason for this is the need to share data between systems and processes, to avoid duplication and consequently improve efficiency. This reflects the drive towards much closer relationships between customers and suppliers advocated at many of the recent conferences on the subject of competitiveness. The trend is encouraged by the concept of open systems being promoted by the main CAD/CAM suppliers. In the creation of an overall IT strategy companies are able to realize the power of the data stored within their CAD/CAM systems, linking them to other processes.

CAD and its partner CAM are well-accepted tools required for success (or even survival) in today's competitive industry. New technology is creating opportunities for the partnership between retailer, manufacturer and designer to become more interdependent and for the combined strengths of a quick response, design aware, market-led team to see off competition from other quarters.

Most companies have a variety of IT systems based primarily on the processing of numeric data (e.g. stock control, payroll, invoicing, etc.). In addition many use PC-based spreadsheets, word processors and databases. Sometimes these are essential tools of the business yet are often contained on a single machine. Often managers fail to realize the ways in which data is stored and manipulated and this is a fundamental weakness in many companies.

A great opportunity exists for a 'switched on' company to enter the field of integrated information systems, where data is the commodity being traded between systems and processes. They can develop a strategy for the evaluation of data requirements throughout the different sites with the goal of providing electronic customer liaison. Indeed, the creation of efficient, flexible, responsive supply chains is the goal of every retailer and the use of IT systems for intercompany data exchange is essential for this to happen.

To achieve this goal two main issues have to be addressed: the quantification of data requirements to define the scope and bandwidth of the networks to be installed and the qualification stage to determine formats, presentation standards, human computer interaction and data access rights.

In 1995 a Radio 4 business programme identified the need for integrated logistics and information technology systems. The conclusion was clear – survival will depend on quick response and this can be efficiently achieved only with accurate up-to-the-minute data. As the whole world may now be viewed as the customer and supplier market it is essential for systems to be interconnected and for managers to liaise with their customers with total confidence in the information being discussed.

The use of IT systems as a means of supplying data to all parts of an organization can, at least initially, be daunting. Managers who have relied on restricted access to figures and plans often find it difficult to adapt to a flatter corporate structure. IT systems can soon justify their contribution to a team approach, using data to assist in planning and to pinpoint bottlenecks in production.

There are, of course, significant cost savings to be made when managers have reliable information on which plans can be developed. The use of computer-based libraries for controlling stock, warehousing and production will provide users with details of availability across different sites and will allow production to be planned to meet customer demand as well as practical production issues. Duplication of stock items would be avoided and time savings, too, may be offered if goods can be shipped between sites rather than manufacturing new ones to order. As benefits are proven the use of data as an enabling mechanism for improving business performance is often a great facilitator of personal culture change.

Part of the need to adopt an IT strategy is as a facilitator of cultural change. The concept of 'information' as a commodity to be shared is an essential shift in attitude that many companies have to adopt. Its use as a means of communication between systems and processes, design and production, customers and suppliers is the means by which change can be made to provide direct benefits in the form of quick response, accurate audits and credible forecasting. The low cost of computing coupled with increasing availability of wide area networks provides a window of opportunity for companies to establish integrated IT systems for use internally and for linking to customers and suppliers. The current use of IT systems in the different parts of many clothing and textiles companies is limited to a few functions with little communication of data between systems and processes. This lack of communication is a regular occurrence in industries that have failed to maintain investment in computer and telecommunications technology or to develop internal staff to maintain or expand systems.

In addition to the development of business systems an information strategy tackles the issues of research and administration and contributes to the generation of an appropriate information culture which understands the necessity for ownership of data, the need to avoid duplication and identify gaps, to ensure accuracy and to guarantee availability.

MANAGEMENT INFORMATION SYSTEMS

Computer technology has been revolutionized since the introduction of the IBM PC in the mid-1980s yet many companies are still using monolithic and cumbersome management systems based on older technology. These systems tend to be inflexible in the format of the data they produce (reports are not well presented) and are frequently awkward to operate (e.g. mistakes have to be corrected by deletion and re-entry rather than on-screen amendment). Most of all these systems tend to be slow and if more than a minimum number of users want concurrent access, they often find that they can enter data faster than the system can acknowledge input. Too often companies will demonstrate the features of their systems by producing large quantities of line printer output only to have to search through this manually for the information they require.

These systems are meant to be aids to business productivity and therefore they are often used to produce management information to assist decision making. The lack of integration with other systems and processes internally means that they are only one source of information necessary for planning. Many of them rely on user input at key stages to produce accurate information, their use not being an integral part of the design and production processes, more an administrative overhead that is not required in these areas. Other problems occur when sales and marketing information is required at the same time as production data. It is rare to find computer systems that are linked and therefore apart from the difference in presentation format there is great potential for data duplication or conflict. A lack of integrated management information is due in large part to the lack of integrated computer systems.

Checklist

- Identify all systems used to produce management information (e.g. sales order processing, invoicing, production, dispatch and stock control)
- Identify the data that is currently produced for managers
- Produce examples of the format used for data presentation
- Establish what data managers would ideally like and in what form
- Review the current computer system(s) to determine compatibility of data formats

ELECTRONIC DATA INTERCHANGE (EDI)

The concept of paperless trading comes one step closer with the requirement set by some retailers for all their suppliers to perform business transactions electronically. To many companies this means the provision of a modem and PC at their own site with a telephone link to the retail headquarters. This step should be only the start and, conducted properly, EDI systems should be used for all transactions with both corporate customers and suppliers. EDI users need to determine the standard they will use for electronic transfer, usually dictated by the customer with whom they are trading, and subscribe to one of many agencies that operate the communications package between organizations.

Checklist

- Identify the number of customers and suppliers with whom transactions could be performed via EDI
- Determine which EDI systems are used by these groups and which system(s) is most appropriate to your business

TELECOMMUNICATIONS

Most companies fail to realize that telecommunications forms an integral part of any IT strategy and many have different telephone systems in each location which lack flexibility. Modern facilities can provide channels for communication of both voice and data (as well as video if necessary) and should form part of an integrated IT strategy. Often 'computer problems' relate to the use of modems or other communications devices rather than the central computer systems.

In many companies the link between computers and telecommunications is effected by the use of a modem, providing an interface to outside parties on a one or two way interrogation process. Often these links are used on a regular (e.g. one daily) basis to transfer key management data between sites. Modems are increasingly used by representatives with portable computers as the link to the home office when they are away from their normal base. The use of a 'dial in' service that enables users to check their e-mail and to transfer data to and from the home system is one way to ensure that an individual's absence from the office causes minimal disruption to the daily workload. This type of connection is replacing the fax and, linked to digital mobile telephones, people can be contacted anywhere in the world.

Provision of the right form of external links to any company's IT network will facilitate highly efficient communications world-wide. There are a variety of telecommunications suppliers and it is worth shopping around to identify the most relevant one: cable companies generally offer better tariffs in the local region but can be more expensive for international calls. High quality lines still cost more than standard ones but can transmit data faster so an increased capital investment may be offset by a decreased running cost.

Checklist

O   Identify what interfaces currently exist between the computer system(s) and the outside world
O   Investigate the nature of the traffic that is generated via external links to assess the quality of line that should be installed
O   Identify all the potential telecommunications suppliers to determine which can supply the most attractive package
O   Consider other options for linking sites, notably on the avoidance of duplicated data and on the improvement of response

SHOP FLOOR DATA

Most factories use a process of self-declaration for operatives to record production and therefore to organize payment (almost all use a piece-rate system). These systems could be replaced by electronic recording using bar-code readers. A great advantage of this type of 'on-line' data recording is the ability to track goods around the shop floor, pinpointing bottlenecks and assisting planning.

In companies with more than one location there is sometimes significant duplication of manufacturing plant, materials stocks and warehousing between the sites. Moreover many design functions are performed in parallel across the factories. The absence of easily accessible records of previous designs, stock items, costing data and assembly instructions leads to repetition and causes unnecessary expense. There is little management understanding of the way that cost can be established as an integral part of the design process.

Many facets of a company's organization have an impact on IT systems: each has its own justification and the purpose of an integrated strategy is to ensure that the key commodity, 'information', is stored and used uniquely and unambiguously.

Checklist

O   Determine what shop floor information is currently generated and how it is used and policed
O   Consider how goods are currently tracked around the factory floor, especially with relationship to servicing enquiries for delivery dates
O   Question the ways in which shop floor data is used in the calculation of costs
O   Confirm what data is passed between different processes in the factory
O   How are labels and tickets used?

WAREHOUSING AND PRODUCTION

The most obvious evidence of computer systems in many companies is seen in the warehouse, the accounts office and the distribution point. Almost all companies use systems to check stock levels, to invoice customers and to produce labels and delivery notes. In many cases this use extends to an integrated financial package that is used for all customer orders and the processing thereof.

Computers for picking and allocating stock, for control of warehouse moving systems and for generation of labels are commonplace in the larger companies. With the move away from very large production runs it is becoming more difficult to justify large control systems. Flexibility is the order of the day and some companies are changing the ways in which their production is organized.

Checklist

O   What IT systems currently exist for these functions?
O   Are these systems integrated and, if not, how is data passed between them?
O   Do the current systems perform all the functions required of them and are they flexible enough to cope with future needs?

SALES ORDER PROCESSING

In many organizations the first use of computer databases was for sales order processing. Systems were used to store orders from customers, to identify and allocate stock, to produce delivery tickets and to generate invoices. These systems were usually capable of storing only text and numbers and often gave output on to pre-formatted computer stationery.

The advent of PC technology has led to a growth in the use of computer databases so that traditional sales order processing functions can now be performed on simple machines, creating the opportunity for systems to be used more creatively and to allow management information to be generated from queries entered into the database. Stock control can be linked automatically to order input and resource planning and costing can also be integrated. Managers can then rely on the availability of up-to-date statistics without the need for time-consuming manual interaction.

Checklist

O   What processes could be linked together under the sales order processing banner?
O   Are there opportunities to integrate stock control and allocation?
O   Can warehouse and delivery functions be incorporated into the sales order processing system?

SECONDARY DESIGN APPLICATIONS

MARKETING AND PROMOTION

A secondary element of design – overlooked by most people – is presentation material: swing tags, labels and packaging as well as marketing and promotional material. CAD/CAM systems can be used to develop ideas for all the ancillary material. In the late 1990s the requirement from the retailers is for manufacturers to give them the 'complete look' and therefore linking all the material that supports a product capitalizes on the knowledge and intelligence that created the original ideas.

In some companies information has to be supplied to the sales and marketing force: the use of CAD/CAM systems can assist in the preparation of samples ahead of mainstream production and can also contribute to catalogues and brochures.

Checklist

O   Can data used for producing a product also be used to create packaging and promotional material?

O   Is there an opportunity to create sales and marketing material to support products from the same source material?

SOURCING AND RESEARCH

In most design studios information exists in the form of magazines, photographs, trend books, newspaper articles, colour charts, notes, retailer briefs and existing garments. It is a complex, ever-changing and often badly organized rag-bag of data. To accommodate the dynamics of the market the system has to cope with seasonal trends and retail requirements. Computer systems have yet to make a significant impact on the supply of data that is gathered from these sources but its arrival is imminent. The Internet is already being used as a source of data and there is a great opportunity to use the latest multimedia computer techniques to present material in a concise form ready for direct use in CAD/CAM systems, saving the time and effort involved in scanning material. In fact Design Intelligence has launched its first CDs containing material that complements its books and slide presentations. *Drapers Record* released its first electronic product 'London Runways on CD' in November 1995.

The FINS project at Nottingham Trent University has been developed for the industry with backing from Nottinghamshire County Council. It is a multimedia database distributed on CD that includes a huge range of information covering sourcing (fabrics, accessories, manufacturers and so on), forecasting (from large and small organizations) and market intelligence (economic data, trends, etc.). The idea behind the project is for companies to be able to use their CAD terminal as an encyclopaedia containing information from as many existing sources as possible, all well organized and beautifully presented.

There is a definite trend towards the use of data from electronic sources and the technical research work necessary to provide payment, to guarantee confidentiality and to offer high performance via the Internet is now becoming available. As companies like BT launch their Integrated Business Systems packages they are linking the concepts of data management, sourcing and design under one umbrella service. As users capitalize on the concepts (which are independent of any particular hardware or software) they will realize the value of their data and their ways of working. The ability to access data that is changed regularly (sometimes every day) will enhance the manufacturer's ability to offer quick response to the retailers who need to ensure their stock will sell.

SYSTEM INTEGRATION

Today there is little full integration of CAD with CAM systems in any company: the majority of CAM systems have been installed solely for the grading, lay planning and cutting processes. As yet few companies are using them for original design work and it is in this area where there will be most growth over the next five years. The full benefits are yet to be realized and cannot be fully identified. Suffice it to say that the sum of the benefits already known at the individual stages will be far less than those that can be obtained from a fully integrated system. It will be the combined capabilities of quality, variety and responsiveness that will drive manufacturers towards the integrated systems approach.

Most companies have IT systems that have grown in an unstructured manner. There are many reasons for this, not least of which is the change in technology that has occurred over the last ten years. Since the mid-1980s PCs have become commonplace and have been able to perform as well (if not better) than the mini and mainframe computers with which they compete. Software has become flexible and uses graphics to improve presentations and thereby makes information available to many.

Often weaknesses start to appear in organizations where this unstructured growth has taken place – often due to duplication of data or inefficient means of transfer between machines. The need for a network becomes essential when such problems arise and therefore companies need to set standards for interchange and need clear management policies for ensuring integrity and availability of data.

There is a tendency to regard IT systems and software as a 'no-go area' where the functions they perform are pre-defined and where output is in set formats. This is where so many businesses fail to capitalize on the real power of the technology: understanding data structures and software functions is the key to the creation of a successful, flexible, IT enabled company that is able to compete with the best in the world. It is also a highly important contributor to administrative efficiency and is therefore one means by which resources (in the form of time and people) can be minimized. Managers therefore need to ensure that they fully understand the power of the technology so that they can list their statements of requirements in a clear and effective manner. Once this is done programmers and engineers can work to produce the results.

As there is so much need for versatility one point must be borne in mind and that is the need for systems to be flexible: software may be able to perform today's functions but it must be designed to cater for tomorrow's needs. The concept of 'open' systems is therefore becoming accepted and this means that data can be exchanged with other systems and processes. It also means that the hardware and software can be updated independently of the data.

Company managers need to plan their IT strategies in much the same manner as they plan production and therefore the starting point is often an audit of existing practices in the creation of the 'information flow' through a company showing how data is passed between people, systems and processes and how computer systems are used to enable this to happen. These strategies should include input from IT suppliers so that product development can be sympathetically integrated into current systems.

Checklist

O   Ensure data is stored without unnecessary duplication and that procedures to avoid accidental replication are adopted

O   Adopt sensible data management policies so that data entry, maintenance and archive activities are properly co-ordinated

O   Perform an 'information audit' on your company to identify data requirements and to scrutinize existing procedures

COST SAVINGS

There are areas of every company where cost savings could be made. The proper use of IT systems is one means by which costs can be identified and plans made on the basis of reliable data. One important area is warehousing where goods ready for shipment to customers represent large amounts of capital. The use of IT recording of goods in stock, in transit and about to enter stock from production can assist managers to plan activities better and to offer customers a quicker response.

Other important areas where IT systems can contribute to cost savings are in the maintenance of libraries of items used in production, notably patterns and fabrics. There is probably significant duplication of stock within most companies and the availability of libraries in the form of pictures as well as textual descriptions would allow managers to plan production in collaboration with suppliers, customers and colleagues.

In some multi-site organizations each location is self-contained except in the areas of finance and distribution. This causes problems when customers ring to chase deliveries and the factory is unable to give direct assistance once goods have left for the warehouse. In other companies the factory is essentially an assembly plant with components purchased on a world-wide basis. This means that improved communications links with all customers and suppliers would be of great value and would save on the administrative costs involved in answering client enquiries.

Checklist

○   Use IT systems to monitor stock accurately throughout the organization and then use the data to improve efficiency

○   Use the computer systems to record all data relating to items in stock and their component parts (i.e. include pictures, illustrations, specification sheets and patterns)

○   Organize an internal filing system so that everyone can understand the benefits of adhering to its structure

○   Investigate the options that exist for improving communications links with customers and suppliers

8

ENABLING TECHNOLOGY

❖

There are numerous reasons why CAD/CAM has so much potential, many of which relate to the availability of inexpensive, highly efficient and very attractive devices for input, output and manipulation. Developments in software and hardware since the late 1980s have occurred at a phenomenal rate and they offer users capability way beyond what could have been achieved before then. Improvements in computer graphic display technology coupled with those in affordable colour printing have enabled creative designers to view CAD not as a novelty with crude lines and poor output but as a set of new media, similar to, but different from, existing techniques. The relatively recent decision by Marks and Spencer to accept design work produced on a computer has lent credibility to CAD; the company's influence spreads throughout the industry and the use of CAD technology is becoming essential.

Most of the new research work in CAD/CAM is going into a limited number of areas, dominated by two topics: multimedia and 3D design. The cost of the hardware required for either of these concepts is now affordable by even the smallest design studios and the increasing availability of high quality telecommunications is driving the market towards distributed computer systems with access from home and office.

The relatively new subject of virtual reality which used to demand high cost, powerful computers is now available for the better PC machines, creating numerous opportunities for the more creative companies to capitalize on the technology as another means of designing and promoting their products.

TECHNOLOGY

Many of the early developments in CAD/CAM technology have been incorporated into other products and provide the foundations for multimedia and

111

virtual reality. In this section current multimedia products are discussed and the problems involved in 3D design and virtual reality are exposed.

MULTIMEDIA

Catalogue shopping is a surprisingly successful part of the clothing business, despite the fact that the companies produce catalogues twice a year and therefore their 'shop window' is fixed for a six-month period. The cost of producing a catalogue is high and it takes a significant time to prepare. Moreover, many of the items on display are photographed from sample merchandise before a main supplier has been sourced.

Multimedia techniques (notably mixing words, diagrams, pictures and music) have the potential to give catalogues a new meaning and a new medium for distribution. The use of interactive CD players coupled with the diversity and power of computer systems makes the idea of a catalogue distributed on disk a possibility. Moreover, when the contents of this disk can combine all the information identified above the package becomes a novel and attractive proposition. When the pictures can move (either in the form of cartoon animation or by replaying short video sequences) and the viewer can control the display and speed of this system many new possibilities emerge.

A few groups are starting to use multimedia technology as a means of promotion and presentation. These applications are likely to grow fast as the CD-ROM gains acceptance as an efficient means of information delivery.

London Runways on CD

One of the first products to hit the market was the 'London Runways on CD' database from *Drapers Record*. This pictorial record of the autumn 1995 London fashion shows is categorized in a comprehensive and easy to access manner. Users of the CD-ROM can ask to see the whole of a designer's collection or can let the system search through all its 700 images for products that featured red as the main colour. The first issue was very well received by the market and set the scene for the distribution of photographic information in an easy to use, simple to search, electronic format. Many novel features were included on the disk including the use of images of rivets as the computer 'buttons' that instruct the software to perform individual searches. One popular feature was the ability to 'zoom in' to any photograph to magnify any part of an image up to 8 times its original size.

Design Intelligence

The forecasting company Design Intelligence has started to put selections of its books on to CD-ROM. It has thus been able to add another dimension to its work, namely using music to enhance the slide shows which form a major part of the CD-ROM contents. Like the London Runways on CD product the creators have included an elegant easy to use interface with buttons to start and stop a slide show, to increase and decrease the volume of the music and to adjust the speed of presentation.

The Storm Model Agency

The Storm Model Agency uses a CD-ROM database as another way of promoting its models. The company is a good example of a business that is thinking creatively about the use of technology. As an agency its role is a broker – introducing client to model – and its commission is earned from bookings. Storm therefore has to promote its models to as wide an audience as possible and so uses multimedia as an additional means of presenting portfolios. Of course the content of the CD-ROM includes video and audio clips, neither of which can be conveyed in the traditional portfolio.

In each of the three cases above the use of multimedia has added a new dimension to the existing work of the companies and has been led by an understanding of market needs. Development in all cases has been designer driven with the computer experts assisting in the detailed technical work. All products have their own unique 'look and feel' and represent the quality and capability of their originators.

Training material

Another very important use of multimedia technology is its application in the training field. Projects are underway at a number of universities (notably Leeds and Manchester) to create material that is used to train users in the basic techniques, terms and methods employed in the design and manufacture of fabrics and textiles. An example of one of the earliest topics to be tackled is the definition of different seam constructions – shown in diagrammatic and photographic form with text descriptions alongside. Some are accompanied by video clips that show how they are formed on specific sewing machines.

Tools like these are helping to train recruits to the industry and can be used in colleges to help students with a wide range of backgrounds to reach a basic level of competence without significant staff involvement. The more advanced products include assessment methods, which enable the computer to record achievement levels of individual users.

FINS – The Fashion Information Service

As discussed in Chapter 7, FINS is a multimedia database created for the clothing and textiles industry. It grew from original research work conducted in Nottinghamshire to investigate the potential of electronic information delivery to designers and manufacturers. The feasibility project involved the participation of groups of users in two areas and their comment and feedback was used to generate the specification of the system.

Unlike many databases FINS relies on the presentation of high quality pictorial information in a well-structured, easy to search format. The primary purpose is to reduce time spent sourcing ideas, identifying suppliers of suitable materials and monitoring the market trends. FINS is very easy to use: most newcomers need only a matter of minutes to gain competence in its 'point and click' method of operation.

FINS runs on standard IBM PC compatible computers and is therefore able to work alongside many of the CAD/CAM packages supplied to the clothing industry. Data can be extracted from FINS and then used in design packages to create new ideas. It can also accept data from other systems. There are three main categories of information in FINS: sourcing, forecasting and market intelligence. Each has a large number of sub-sections, each categorized so that data is easy to find.

Sourcing data covers the suppliers of yarns and fabrics, trimmings and accessories as well as garment producers. It lists agents and has a section called the 'capacity register' which gives company details that include manufacturing capacity, specialist skills and market position. For example, users can search for a company that makes swimwear and operates on a cut, make and trim (CMT) basis. It includes printers, dyers and finishers and has sections on machinery suppliers (including CAD/CAM) and on distribution services.

Forecasting information comes from a variety of sources: some of the commercial companies like Design Intelligence provide their material in slide show form; the yarn and fibre suppliers have their own material based on storyboards and colour themes and the trade bodies link ideas together in manners that are both creative and highly visual.

Market intelligence information includes reports on shows and conferences from round the world and also has regularly updated sales information, indicating what is selling on the high street. Commercial market research companies use FINS as a means of showing how they operate and how their output can assist companies to capitalize on business opportunities, especially in mid-season manufacture.

FINS is available in CD-ROM format and is issued 10 times each year. It is the most comprehensive database in the UK and is also the subject of trials with organizations all over Europe to investigate the potential of new telecommunications links so that every item can be updated 'on-line', ensuring that it reflects ever-changing trends. It is unlikely that this service will be affordable by the majority of small companies until 1998 or 1999 as the cost of the high-grade telecommunications lines will be too high until then.

FINS may be regarded as a brokerage service, linking suppliers and customers. It builds into an archive: the validity of last year's forecasts can be checked against today's sales and this can help users to determine which sources are most useful to their own business. FINS can also be used as a bureau service and this is one way in which companies can have access without making any hardware or software investment themselves. There is an increasing number of centres where FINS can be accessed and in most of them links to CAD/CAM systems can be demonstrated.

MEASURING SYSTEMS

One of the oldest problems in the made-to-measure market is the need to take a comprehensive, accurate set of measurements for each client. This process requires skill and takes time, both of which are in short supply. The Telmat measuring booth system at Nottingham Trent University (see Figure 8) uses a photographic silhouette technique to identify human form and sophisticated shape recognition software to identify body elements from which measurements are calculated. This system has the great advantage of being fast to use (measurements are available in two minutes) and is accurate enough for clothing to be manufactured to the figures it reports.

Similar systems using laser technology are available in the USA and Japan, each creating a 3D contour map of the subject. A measuring booth manufactured by the Japanese company Hammamatsu is now available to capture full 3D

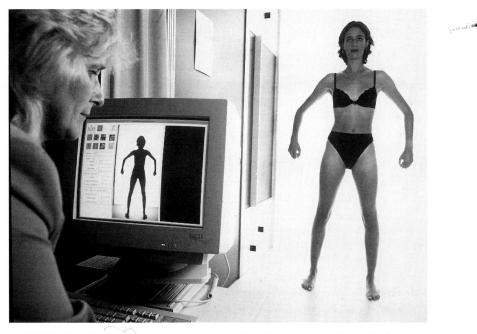

FIGURE 8   Telmat measuring booth (© James King-Holmes)

surface data. The process takes less than one minute and creates a full 3D model of the subject. Work at University College London is being undertaken to write software that will automatically create measurements of each individual.

At the time of writing all these are expensive options (costing over £50 000 each) but their use on a hire basis is becoming accepted practice. Linking their output with virtual reality systems is the natural progression for companies entering the field of 3D modelling.

3D

To date almost all systems have performed operations in two dimensions (patterns have been manipulated in their flat form and photographs have been used as the background for image manipulation and display). The next big developments will be in the use of 3D for both patterns and displays and this will encompass the use of virtual reality as a means of representation and interaction.

As the use of CAD, multimedia and remote working increases, the need for even better communications will grow, especially in the competition between firms. Two-dimensional designs will become less desirable than 3D: once one company is able to show a garment in its 3D form then all the others will follow suit. As yet 3D represents unexploited potential, mainly because the creation of good models (human and garment) is difficult and requires a mixture of artistic and scientific knowledge. Other industries (notably automotive and aerospace) have been 3D users for some time, using models to simulate, to calculate and to create. The clothing industry's needs are different – the primary role of any system is to communicate design ideas and concepts to retail buyers and this implies realistic simulation and interactive creation: it does not demand analytical calculation. Aesthetic considerations are more important than mathematical exactness – a key point to note when considering the very difficult problems of creating accurate models with flexible fabrics.

Animating a 3D object is a separate problem – synthetic movement of a humanoid is very difficult to create but is essential if garments are to be shown in a realistic manner on models in the required poses. Garments themselves are complex items requiring careful assembly in the computer system before they can be draped around a human form. Although modelling is a daunting process it does have enormous attractions and as the techniques become more refined so libraries of animated humans will become available enabling companies to purchase a computerized 'Naomi Campbell' on which their goods can be displayed.

Human modelling

Almost all the attempts at modelling the human form have been based on surface scanning techniques to create a map of the body in contour form which is subsequently texture mapped to give it a skin. Loughborough University has been a pioneer in this body measuring technique and has developed a rig that can create an accurate 3D model of a human being in a few minutes. Cyberware in the USA has developed a similar process and can measure a complete body but on a system costing about $250 000. Its best known work is based around the movie industry and it is to Hollywood that we have to look for the most dramatic effects in computer modelling of people. Just think of the film *Terminator 2* to realize the mixture of modelling techniques that are available.

The research team at Nottingham Trent University are using the Telmat system to perform shape analysis, incorporating posture and figuration into their work on clothing patterns, and are extracting the data in 3D form to display mannequins that reflect both the size and shape of individual subjects.

One of the obvious elements of the human form (even of the top models) is our inherent imperfection – our left and right sides are not symmetrical, we have different amounts of body hair (in the right and wrong places!), we have cuts, bruises, warts and moles – in fact we are seriously flawed. The process of putting a skin on a computerized model needs to account for these little imperfections before wholly realistic beings can be made.

The most fundamental problem is in creating realistic human forms that move in a convincing manner. Our actions are controlled by our muscles, which move the bones to which they are anchored and animate our flesh. Almost all systems model humans from a surface scan, yet nature builds from the inside out, starting with a skeleton and adding muscle, fat and skin. The inner body is totally ignored by a surface scanning approach. It is to X-rays and ultrasonic probes that we have to look before a skeleton can be seen in relation to the covering fat, flesh and skin. It is the combination of all these factors that helps us to understand movement and it is from the medical and sports worlds that basic information will be derived on which computerized movement in 3D can be created.

Even when we understand all the mechanics of movement we need to add 'personality' – when thinking of a catwalk show we need to understand how models accentuate their natural movements to enhance the garments that they wear.

Constructing in 3D

Fashion designers tend to be artistic rather than scientific in their approach to problem solving. Their ability to model in 3D is geared wholly to the dress stand: ask them to read an engineering drawing showing plan, view and elevation and they are scuppered. As yet we have neither a 3D input device nor a 3D display and these limitations will be off-putting if not insurmountable barriers to the effective use of today's technology.

Modelling cloth

The problem of accurate representation of flexible materials on a computer screen remains one of the most fundamental left to solve. It is important to limit the problem to artistic constraints.

A lot of work has been done in this area with UK bodies taking a leading role. Most of the theories have been based on 'finite element analysis' techniques and although these work well for simple fabrics wrapped around even complex shapes they fail to produce sensible effects with complex, jointed materials. David Lloyd at Bradford University has pioneered much of this work yet he has had enormous difficulty in attracting funds for research. The complexity of the mathematics involved in this field is off-putting to many interested parties!

VIRTUAL REALITY

To many the term 'virtual reality' conjures up visions of computer whiz-kids looking ridiculous in space helmets, pointing at invisible objects with cumbersome looking gloves connected by wires to computers. Some may even have tried VR systems in the games arcades. This type of 'immersion' experience, displaying images on small screens located in the space helmet in front of each eye, is alien to most people. Recently available is the type of 'desktop' VR system that uses a standard computer monitor to display the images in the 'virtual world'. This has a number of advantages over the immersion systems: it is less expensive, gives higher quality pictures and allows existing technology to be used for its control and development. In fact it opens virtual reality to a whole host of applications.

The advent of virtual reality heralds a new era in design possibilities. It offers a seductive package of goodies suggesting that a computerized catwalk show is feasible, with animated models and flowing garments, giving the viewer the option to see the show from any position and providing the ultimate in efficient communications. Its potential extends far outside the supplier/retailer relationship – it will appeal even to the high fashion market, offering variety and innovation to the traditional catwalk show. To capitalize on its potential the clothing and textiles market needs to embrace 3D as an unavoidable step on the path to a virtual catwalk show.

NETWORKS

THE INTERNET

The best known network is the 'Internet' or 'World Wide Web'. For a very low price customers can connect their own computers to others all round the world simply by plugging a modem into the local telephone network and linking their computer to one of a variety of system providers. Millions of companies and individuals have created their own promotional material (known as 'pages') so that their content can be viewed by anyone with a similar connection. The spectacular growth of the Internet, starting in the early 1990s, has been at the centre of the information revolution.

The first clothing companies to put details of their products on the Internet, Griffin Laundry and Walter Van Beirendonck, gained significant exposure in a variety of media: not only were their products being seen by large numbers of Internet users, the methods they were using had such novelty value that articles were written about the companies in dozens of journals.

The main limitation of the Internet is the speed at which it operates – users often have to wait a long time for information to be displayed on their screens, dependent both on the quality of telecommunications line and the number of users at any time. This means that the fastest response is gained from sources that include only a small number of images (pictures, graphics or video clips) and where text is the main content.

In the fast changing world of fashion there is an ever-present need to keep up to date with the latest trends. The use of books, CD-ROMS and magazines is commonplace but these take time to produce and distribute. The same information published on the Internet is instantly available world-wide and can be amended frequently. Consequently there is an increasing demand from the clothing and textiles industry for data sourced from the Internet.

The use of search mechanisms to assist users in the quick selection of data is invaluable and there are many ways in which data from the Internet can be accessed in easy to find, ready to use form. Although most searches are conducted using words there is scientific research in companies like IBM to provide the mechanics by which colour and shape can be used to access electronic libraries of data, be they on CD-ROM or the Internet. Some of these tools will be invaluable to the creative designers who often think in aesthetic terms.

LOCAL AREA NETWORKS

The most common networks in companies today are those based around a set of PCs linked to one or more central file servers to form a local area network (LAN). The machines are connected either via a 'daisy chain', one machine being linked via a cable to the next, or on a 'star' configuration where each machine is connected to a central hub.

LANs effectively allow users to share information by permitting them to access data held on the central server. Individuals can manipulate data, create their own information and experiment with packages without impact on other users and only when they deem the time to be right do they place their results on the central server for others to access.

PCs themselves can be used as 'terminal emulators' and this means that they can talk to the older, mini and mainframe computer systems by direct connection to the networks that enable them to function. Many companies now adopt the policy of upgrading their computer systems strategically, replacing 'dumb terminals' with PCs as the former become obsolete or not worth repairing.

Companies like Benetton have state-of-the-art plants where all systems are connected together in a 'techno village' concept. All users have the ability to send and receive data in the form of pictures, photographs, voice and video: a truly integrated design environment. Most LAN users appreciate the flexibility, efficiency and speed of communications available to them and the simple ability to share peripheral devices (printers, plotters, scanners, etc.) offers significant time savings and optimizes the use of infrequently used hardware.

WIDE AREA NETWORKS

Whatever is done on a local area network (normally within one site) can also be done over a large geographic area. To create a wide area network (WAN) links have to be established with remote establishments, via BT or a similar telecommunications supplier. This means that the cabling is either rented on a direct connect basis (a 'private wire') or uses the existing telephone system to provide the link (a 'switched system'). The former has the advantage that it costs very little to run once it has been installed but has the disadvantage that it can be used only between the two nominated points. The latter can, of course, be used to connect anywhere in the world and is cheap to install but the call charges are based on the amount of use and can seem high.

Obviously the need for a WAN must be justified on the amount of interaction that occurs between sites, but WANs do offer many advantages. Any data that is normally sent by courier, mail or other means can be transferred electronically, ensuring minimal delivery time and reducing the amount of manpower used in the process of off-loading the data (writing to tape or disk) and re-loading at the far end.

New technologies like video conferencing require the WAN concept and can be used to save time and travel. Designers can confer with each other, sharing data as well as seeing their partners in video form, thus adopting CSCW (Computer Supported Collaborative Working) principles (see p. 34). An example of this may be in the connection of a buyer in London to a designer in Milan. The two can be talking on the telephone about a garment design that is simultaneously seen on computer screens in both locations. Changes made by the designer can be reviewed by the buyer and agreement can be effected without the need for travel or samples.

The amount of traffic and the speed of response required by users will determine the quality (expressed in terms of 'bandwidth') of the lines needed to connect parties together. The late twentieth century is witnessing a staggering growth in bandwidth capacity both to the home (evident in the rapid expansion of cable TV and telephone services) and to business and educational establishments. The relatively slow response speed of the Internet, the prime example of a world-wide wide area network, demonstrates the problems that occur when only limited bandwidth is available. Indeed, this emphasizes the point that bandwidth has to be shared between all users and if everyone requires simultaneous access to common data the response speed will go down.

Perhaps the first reason for connecting to other users is to exchange information and this is frequently achieved by connecting two users together using a modem at each end, plugging each computer into the public telephone network. This method has the advantage of being inexpensive but is relatively slow and can be used only when relatively small quantities of data are required. Connecting remote users to LANs or two LANs together is the general concept of a wide area network and most system managers aim to provide the highest possible quality of transmission between sites. Bandwidth is generally available in multiples of 64 kb/s or one ISDN telephone line. To offer a remote user the equivalent of a LAN connection 160 of these lines would be needed!

Developments in wide area network technology are occurring at a tremendous pace and their availability will increase dramatically as their cost decreases.

9

WHERE IS IT ALL GOING?

❖

CAD/CAM systems are improving all the time, capitalizing on the price and performance of the latest computer hardware and software. Vendors are forever adding to their range of functions in a constant attempt to be the most effective supplier to the market.

Chapter 8 gives an outline of the major developments in technology that are going to affect CAD/CAM systems in clothing and textiles. They have a significant role to play in shortening the time it takes to go from product concept to shipment by reducing the number of iterative loops in negotiation between customer and supplier. Their use as a communication tool is vital – computer screens are the windows through which design information may be viewed in a variety of forms (graphic images, specification sheets, costing estimates, assembly instructions and so forth). Within the context of an integrated IT environment CAD/CAM systems are going to play an increasingly important role.

CAD/CAM IN OTHER INDUSTRIES

Clothing and textiles companies' use of CAD/CAM is less developed than many other industry sectors. They can, however, benefit from the lessons learned by others. A few examples are discussed below as a guide to the type of functions that the technology can perform.

In architecture and building companies CAD was first used as a direct replacement for the drawing board. Its justification was the minimization of time taken to create drawings, especially when libraries of components (e.g. windows, doors and roof joists) were created. Once established they were able to give a consistency to drawings. Systems were also used to make amendments, dispensing with the need to re-create drawings when corrections could not be made to the original.

All of the initial functions were performed in 2D – just like manual methods. Once CAD was generally accepted the industry became aware of the benefits that 3D can offer and systems are now used to create models of buildings in both wire frame and solid form. Draughtsmen and women have had to acquire modelling skills but the benefits are manifold, especially when the output is used to convey to customers the effect a completed building will have to the eye. Naturally CAD/CAM systems can extract 2D views to replicate the traditional methods but the 3D object is seen as a superior device.

The military establishment has consistently invested in high technology and it can be credited with much of the development work that has contributed to today's computer facilities. Much of its work has been in the field of image representation, piecing together satellite pictures to identify missile sites and the like. Graphics are used to process images and to highlight the parts that are of strategic importance and so many of the photographic processing techniques now available in PC-based packages were first used in command and control applications. Many commonplace computer paintbox functions also originated in military establishments. The aerospace industry uses such techniques as well and used 3D CAD to assist in the simulation of flight, employing sophisticated mathematical packages to monitor air flow, stability and forces on aircraft and rockets.

Engineers, too, are heavy users of CAD/CAM: electronics experts rely on the technology to design microchips and to lay out components on the printed circuit boards that are contained in all computers and many domestic appliances. Mechanical and civil engineers use systems for draughting, modelling and simulation.

Perhaps the most glamorous industry that uses computer-aided systems is film and television. Some of the most memorable elements of films like *Jurassic Park* were created using both 2D and 3D modelling techniques. Other groups (notably those led by Daniel and Nadia Thalmann in Switzerland) specialize in the creation of computer-generated movies. Advertisers, too, were quick to capitalize on the technology to create effects that were not possible by other means. The creative energy of the media quarter is a driving force in the use of CAD and it is one from which clothing and textiles designers can learn a great deal.

CAD/CAM is now established at all levels of the clothing and textiles industry – the original investment has justified its payback and systems are proliferating in retailers, manufacturers and design offices – but many companies could still benefit much more from the technology.

RETAILERS

Retailers are looking to computer technology as an important contributor to business success. They are starting to exploit the technology as a means of communicating with their suppliers, reducing the amount of paperwork involved in any transaction and improving their response time. Some companies, such as Marks and Spencer (see p. 98), are even setting standards whereby their suppliers are instructed to install certain items of equipment so that transactions can be performed by EDI methods.

Retailers are also looking to the technology to provide many other benefits and products like PDM from Gerber are setting standards for the assembly of information relating to garments in a multimedia, integrated manner. In fact the concept of an integrated product data management system is being embraced by many retailers and larger manufacturers. The opportunities to reduce duplicate activity, to provide central libraries of material including fabrics, patterns and accessories as well as size charts and sales figures are becoming highly attractive. Data warehouses are being created in many retail headquarters to provide both a strategic resource for managers and planners (sales patterns can be linked to historical trends) and a source of information for designers.

By using integrated computer systems retailers are able to issue standard pattern blocks, grading rules and the like to all their suppliers, guaranteeing accurate and consistent garment sizes across a range of manufacturers. This in turn is leading to reduced sampling (manufacturers are more likely to get it right first time) and improved fit (assuming the retailers have created their own size charts correctly).

The generic ideas embraced by the Marks and Spencer Contract Management System will be adopted by all other retailers over the next few years. It demands a more open approach to data, with many transactions being made by electronic means, and suppliers must therefore know exactly how data can be exchanged with the retailers and will be influential in the creation of an open systems approach.

Companies such as Dolcis (with their Project 100) and BhS (with the Breakthrough initiative) are aiming to increase their turnover with a reduced supply base. This means that their suppliers will have to offer both manufacturing capacity and design flair. The reliable, flexible, quick response culture will prevail and this in turn will demand efficient communications.

Some retailers are stipulating that their suppliers be 'design management led companies'. This proviso requires manufacturers to undertake significant planning of their product offer and to identify markets, customer perceptions and fashion trends to increase their value to their customers. They will also have to develop improved strategies for guaranteeing delivery and this may be aided by computer packages for critical path analysis and factory planning and simulation.

As systems like the Telmat measuring booth (see p. 115) become more widely used there will be an increased understanding of 'fit' and many retailers will be using the technology coupled to their CAD/CAM systems to produce made-to-measure goods or to conduct regular sizing surveys.

There are many other ways in which computer systems are starting to be used by retailers. 3D design and virtual reality packages are being used to create store layouts that are used to assist in planning the most effective distribution of display stands, cash points and changing rooms. Promotional material, colour schemes and packaging ideas can all be explored with the technology and CAD is a vital part of this process.

Some organizations are using the Internet or World Wide Web to promote their products. The initial value is probably not in an increase in sales that are directly attributable to the advertisements but more an indirect contribution to awareness of the company and its products in a market that may not have known about them before.

All of the ideas covered in this book are being embraced by the retailers but few have either the resources or the knowledge to integrate them all.

CUSTOMERS

IN-STORE SYSTEMS

Customers are already starting to see how computer technology can be used in retail stores. The use of electronic point of sales (EPOS) cash terminals that read the bar codes on the goods being purchased is familiar and the benefits of detailed receipts are obvious. Less clear to customers is the way in which the resulting data is used to assist retailers to identify the most popular sizes, the best selling goods and the mix of colours that are selling best. It is this data that helps retailers ensure that the right mix of goods is available in store to fulfil customer demands.

There are so many opportunities for companies to use IT systems at the point of sale and in the selling/buying process. Computer touch-screens in some of the large department stores show shoppers the location of goods, and multimedia catalogues, Internet shops and television shopping are all available. These developments are all new to the retail environment and have yet to establish credibility but some of them will survive and become big business. Clothing and textiles companies therefore need to learn how to use the power of these systems to increase their turnover and capitalize on the opportunities the technology can offer.

PERSONAL SERVICE

Perhaps the biggest problem for high street customers is the problem of 'fit'. It is not unusual for a woman to have garments in her wardrobe labelled from a size 8 to a size 14 depending on the style of garment and the shop from which it was purchased. The measuring technology that is emerging from the research laboratories means that computers can create a full three-dimensional model of each customer and put this on to a disk or smart card. By giving one of these cards to each customer a retail store can develop a much closer relationship with its clients.

A typical scenario might be that when a customer enters a store he or she plugs their own card into the in-store computer which then recommends the correct size of any garment to fit the individual. The computer would simply identify from its database of the current in-store clothes which is the best size for each part of the customer's body. It could recommend a size 12 top and a size 14 trouser or a size 16 skirt depending on the style of garment and the particular manufacturer. Indeed, some stores will want to remove the '12', '14' and '16' size system and replace them with 'C', 'D' and 'E' or 'Petite', 'Upright, tall' and 'Mature'. The primary benefit to customers will be the ability to purchase goods that fit better without the psychologically difficult realization that 'I'm a size 14 rather than a size 12.' Indeed, a very important new market may emerge, namely a 'made-to-measure' service. With smart cards containing full customer size and shape details it is possible to request a company to manufacture clothes for the individual customer without the need for fittings. Personalization will become a means of setting individual style and obtaining better fit.

As retailers exploit their knowledge of individual buying preferences gained from the bar-coding on goods and the use of credit and debit cards it is likely that shopping in even the biggest stores will become a more personal process. There will be a trend towards more personalization and this in turn will generate brand loyalty.

ELECTRONIC CATALOGUES FOR HOME SHOPPING

A completely different aspect of the use of the technology will be the increasing number of sales catalogues being put on to CD-ROM. As this technology takes off and is linked to increasingly sophisticated databases customers will be targeted with products appropriate to their age, lifestyle and buying habits. These databases may include details of a customer's size and shape and this may help to overcome the problem of goods returned due to the selection of the wrong size: companies will be able to match the label in the garment to the measurements of the client rather than relying on hand measuring or wishful thinking on the part of the client!

This use of databases is a whole new concept in direct mailing and has exciting possibilities for more personalized service using data collected over a period of time to understand customer trends and spending patterns.

Some of this work is already being undertaken as data warehouses are being created by the high street retailers.

ON-LINE SHOPPING

Once CD-ROM is well accepted and as cable TV companies offer computer connections in addition to their standard services there will be a move to provide catalogues on an 'on-line, dial-in' service. This will have big benefits: customers will be able to see the very latest goods (on-line data can be amended daily) and will be able to check stock levels from their home computer terminal; orders can be input direct from the home without the need to speak to an operator; and, of course, the system will be available 24 hours a day, seven days per week.

The use of digital television operated interactively is going to be the way in which large numbers of consumers will access on-line shopping without the need for their own computer. The full impact of this type of shopping experience is yet to be realized but Bill Gates, chief executive of Microsoft, estimates that one-third of American shopping malls will close by the end of the century due to the rise in popularity of on-line shopping.

MANUFACTURERS

To some extent manufacturers are being driven down the technology path by retailers. This is a sceptical view and it may be fairer to suggest that retailers are attempting to set standards that others will follow. The output from many manufacturers supplies a very limited number of retail customers. Some manufacturers even produce for a single customer. It is therefore essential to ensure that business links with these clients are founded on strong principles. As retailers demand ever more responsive and flexible manufacture so they are streamlining their administrative procedures to ensure that their requirements from the suppliers are matched by their own organizational processes.

Manufacturing companies use many reasons to justify their investment in CAD/CAM yet some fail to capitalize on the full potential of the technology. Often systems are used for a limited set of tasks, each perfectly valid, yet frequently not linked to other systems or processes. Therefore the initial development task for many manufacturers is to provide links to their CAD/CAM systems so that data can be received from retailers in electronic form and sent back in a similar manner. The adoption of standards often means that data can be exchanged between systems and processes internally as well as to the outside world and this has a great benefit to the efficiency of internal communications. As communications improve so the benefits of a flexible workforce, a talented design team, an increased awareness of market needs and an aggressive sales team can be realized. All these factors combine to give companies a competitive advantage over those who fail to capitalize on the true power of information technology systems.

As links are exploited so there is a greater opportunity for manufacturers to create reputations for innovative design work, flexible manufacture and reliable delivery with consistently high quality standards. The increased interaction between manufacturers and retailers will facilitate the development of strategic development teams both inter and intra company so that market trends can be analysed and used to develop new ranges as a collaborative design process between buyer and designer. Both parties should benefit from closer ties, capitalizing on the strength of their combined knowledge and employing the skills of the production teams in making goods on a 'just in time' principle.

Most companies use their CAD/CAM systems wisely and an increasing number are realizing that the systems can be employed in lateral ways in the promotion and presentation of their products. In this field companies are starting to produce electronic catalogues showing their goods in multimedia form. These systems can be used as interactive order pads when installed on portable computers and used in the salesperson/customer environment. Other companies involve their customers in the design process, again taking the technology out to the customer's site and working with the individual client on the final stages of design, thereby involving potential purchasers in the creative phase and gaining their commitment to a product before a sample is made. The psychology of the buying and selling process can be exploited by sensible use of CAD/CAM systems.

Some manufacturers have recognized the benefits of closer working relationships and are forming links with their computer suppliers, offering advice on new functionality and features that would assist in the design and production processes. As test sites they offer suppliers an excellent opportunity to prove the effectiveness of each new software or hardware tool and benefit from being ahead of their competitors when new versions are issued. To this extent manufacturers are forming collaborative design teams with their suppliers, mimicking those they develop with their customers.

Of course, systems are not just used in the design room and as multimedia applications grow it will be increasingly common to see computer screens throughout the production area, using the electronic medium to demonstrate new techniques for assembly or instruct on safety or quality standards. They will also be used to monitor production: bar-code readers will identify when garments pass strategic points in the process, allowing accurate information on manufacturing times, operator performance and work in progress to be extracted.

Stock control packages are relatively commonplace but are rarely linked to other systems and processes. Manufacturing staff will see an increasing use of integrated IT systems as a means of planning production and minimizing the amount of capital tied up in stock. The concepts of 'just in time' manufacture will apply equally to all other activities.

Managers are going to see a vast increase in their use of IT systems as a means of planning. They must be able to plan for all eventualities and be flexible enough to cope with ever-changing markets and volatile economies. A good IT system will assist in problem solving and strategic planning.

Clothing and textiles companies have generally been slow to embrace computer technology and have fallen behind other sectors. The European Union and the Department of Trade and Industry have both recognized this situation and are actively encouraging firms in the market sector to apply for grants (usually 50 per cent of costs) to help bring them up to date and enhance competitiveness. For example, the DTI has launched an 'Information Society Initiative' as a means of promoting the value of technology to small and medium-sized companies. Grants are available for innovation, research and technology transfer. Being willing to invest in new equipment or to exploit existing facilities under the umbrella of a research programme means that companies can be eligible for grants: those without the technology cannot apply.

DESIGNERS

Almost all design work in clothing and textiles is performed in two dimensions – CAD/CAM systems have excellent facilities for manipulating data and presenting it in concise, visually attractive ways. The opportunity exists for design and production personnel to work in closer collaboration, each with access to the design information, in a way that streamlines the transition from concept to product. To enable this to happen they will each require access to the central data store (almost certainly via a network) and protocols need to be developed so that each can view and amend data in a manner suited to their own job. This process is particularly beneficial to organizations where personnel are not located in the same place. Depending on the nature of the separation the interconnection may be via a local or a wide area network.

To use electronic communication efficiently between design and production a far more detailed study into the tools, timescales and methods needs to be undertaken. Time should be spent on an investigation to identify the current practices and to establish local rationales for existing methods. Only against this background can improvements be recommended with confidence and with the support of staff in each location.

As computer hardware and software becomes more complex there is an opportunity for systems to be used to represent 3D data and to use newer software products like virtual reality. 3D design in clothing has to consider all the functions required to wrap and unwrap 3D shapes, turning them back into 2D flat patterns and then back again into 3D: in the late twentieth century this task is feasible but difficult. The modelling of humans is improving at speed and work at Loughborough, UCL and Nottingham Trent Universities on measuring 3D forms accurately and quickly is leading the world in full-scale body detailing. This has the potential to be linked to animation and VR systems permitting a wealth of accurate, aesthetically pleasing human forms to be created.

It is likely that more designers will take to the technology when a library of human models is available and a straightforward method of putting pattern pieces on to these dummies via a computer interface has been developed. We will need methods of pinning and tucking before the creation of 3D garments becomes simple.

SUPPLIERS

CAD/CAM technology is going to make a significant impact on suppliers of goods to all parts of the supply chain. The most obvious contribution will be in the use of electronic catalogues, put on to portable computers for salespeople to demonstrate to their clients or on to CD-ROM for distribution and playback on customers' own machines. No longer will salespeople need to drive a car load of stock around.

The portable system will contain an electronic catalogue showing the full range of stock combining photographs, diagrams, illustrations, video, text, music and commentary. The salesperson will guide potential customers through the company's range and the computer system will offer features such as the ability to zoom in to a photograph to inspect part in more detail. The salesperson will have order forms ready on the system so that all paperwork can be conducted on screen with paper transactions eliminated. By plugging the computer into a nearby telephone socket the computer can automatically check stock availability and confirm delivery times.

ORGANIZATIONS

The many pressures on companies to organize themselves efficiently have led to much flatter management structures with minimal hierarchies. In practice this has meant that CAD/CAM systems are exposed to managers and directors and their use is often questioned at the top level. It is fair to say that some users fail to exploit the power of their systems and often this is because the original purchase was incorrectly justified. There is an increasing trend towards more flexible manufacture which will require highly flexible IT systems.

CHANGING STRUCTURES

The trend towards flatter organizational structures is demanding a cultural change within businesses with responsibility being delegated. The term 'empowerment' is becoming synonymous with management change. Changes in management structure coupled with changes in work practice (notably the introduction of teamworking) mean that companies are having to review many of their business and organizational practices. This is providing a good reason for the review of IT systems, including CAD/CAM, in the context of a need for greater productivity and responsiveness.

VIRTUAL ORGANIZATIONS

Companies with more than one location can use some of the new technology to overcome geographical barriers and allow themselves to be viewed as one 'virtual organization' where the location of any office is of little importance. This concept is growing quickly in organizations with multiple sites (often including international partners) and is the subject of studies being undertaken by the DTI as part of its CSCW (Computer Supported Collaborative Working) programme.

One realization of the effectiveness of a networked organization is the creation of a group-wide telephone directory organized by names, function, experience and so on. The IT element of this is simple and when the directory is linked to the telephone system the desktop PC becomes the desktop communications console with dialling and connection an integral part of the system.

PERSONNEL

The use of IT systems to provide corporate summaries of human resources is another example of the virtual organization. It should be possible to identify discrepancies in existing payment structures and to analyse throughput and productivity times from any location. The personnel department should be a user of any IT system. As skills requirements change it is the role of personnel to identify ways in which existing skills can be utilized without the need to lose staff. There is still a shortage of qualified graduates coming into the industry with both experience and computer skills and therefore there is a great opportunity for retraining internal staff in the new technology, making a positive contribution to Continuing Professional Development (CPD) as well as setting the company down the track of Investors in People (IIP) accreditation.

RESEARCH GROUPS

Many institutions have reputations based on specialist skills and facilities and these bodies act as centres of excellence in their own fields. Some have groups like textile testing laboratories that complement pure research activity but are essential to the industry and enhance an institution's reputation. Traditionally, however, there has been little cohesion between organizations. The reorganization of higher education funding and the intervention of the Department of Trade and Industry is creating a new culture of research in the field of clothing and textiles with CAD/CAM topics high on the agenda. Institutions are being encouraged to collaborate and different disciplines are providing complementary views on research topics.

Universities and research organizations are creating teams with mixed backgrounds, mixing arts and science skills to develop greater understanding of the problems encountered when trying to use IT systems to simulate the manufacture of clothing and to represent accurately the aesthetics and mechanics of people, cloth and garments. Research activities (which have traditionally focused on the engineering and science disciplines) are now encompassing art and design aspects as well as the social sciences. Interaction with industry is being encouraged as a means of ensuring the commercial viability of research and development activity.

Colleges house a variety of CAD/CAM systems, many used for undergraduate teaching but some reserved for specialist research activity. As each institution has justified their purchase on the grounds of suitability for research there is a wealth of practical experience of systems within the academic sector. But, while knowledge of the performance of particular hardware and software packages is sound, the lack of real production work in academic environments means that experience is limited. Some teams have evaluated human-computer interfaces, others the time-saving potential, while some have specialized in the design capability of systems and their use as a creative medium.

The increasing acceptance that the introduction of new technology into a company must often be accompanied by a change in culture means that the social, economic and psychological aspects of the introduction of IT are also a topic for university research. The independence of the institutions and the objectivity of their researchers may make them an attractive source of information to companies wishing to invest and prepare themselves for the new century. The clothing and textiles industry can look forward to increased research activity in the future.

CONCLUSION

The increasing use of CAD/CAM and associated tools will allow designers to work anywhere in the world and remain in contact with their market. Some areas will be able to rediscover their historic roots and capitalize on their reputation as centres of excellence. Catalogues will be published in electronic form offering views round 'virtual galleries' and 'computerized fashion shows' at the customer's desk. Archives will be dusted down, catalogued and reproduced in CD-ROM or on-line form so that they can be used to influence the new designers in the traditional manner of learning from our forebears. 'Nottinghamshire lace' and 'Irish linen' will no longer be anachronisms but will signify the history and knowledge in those areas.

The end of the twentieth century sees the cyclic pattern observed so often in the fashion industry coming full circle. In the last 100 years we have witnessed the demise of the personal tailor and dressmaker and the creation of the mass market clothing industry. Specialist stores have been in decline as the multiples have expanded. Yet consumer tastes are changing and as modern computer technology spreads into the home it offers a wonderful opportunity for much closer relationships between individual customers and their suppliers.

There will be new business opportunities as designers establish themselves as 'on-line image advisers' operating businesses that offer consultancy services to individuals and companies alike. Personalization of design will become big business as the new century unrolls and it is those businesses that identify and capitalize on the potential of IT that will thrive. Collaborative design based on sound trading principles will become an ordinary concept and this in turn will increase the general public's perception of the value of clothes.

It is those designers, manufacturers, retailers and suppliers who grasp the technology, who make it work creatively as well as capitalizing on its ability to perform mundane tasks quickly, accurately and effectively who will be the driving force behind British clothing manufacture in the twenty-first century. It will become apparent that the new experts will be those users who combine artistic talent with a sound understanding of scientific principles. The millennium heralds an exciting era – a true mixing of art and science: it remains to be seen who will be the Leonardo da Vinci of the technological world.